The Rules of the Game

The Rules of the Game

A Guide to Writing in Standard English

Philip J. Skerry

ROWMAN & LITTLEFIELD
Lanham • Boulder • New York • London

Published by Rowman & Littlefield
An imprint of The Rowman & Littlefield Publishing Group, Inc.
4501 Forbes Boulevard, Suite 200, Lanham, Maryland 20706
www.rowman.com

6 Tinworth Street, London SE11 5AL

Copyright © 2019 by Philip J. Skerry

All rights reserved. No part of this book may be reproduced in any form or by any electronic or mechanical means, including information storage and retrieval systems, without written permission from the publisher, except by a reviewer who may quote passages in a review.

British Library Cataloguing in Publication Information Available

Library of Congress Cataloging-in-Publication Data Available

ISBN 978-1-4758-5296-7 (cloth)
ISBN 978-1-4758-5297-4 (pbk.)
ISBN 978-1-4758-5298-1 (electronic)

For Jules Ryckebusch and Dan Miller:
teachers, mentors, friends

Contents

Preface: What Is Standard Written American English (SWAE)?	ix
Acknowledgments	xi
Introduction: Why Writers Have Difficulty with SWAE	1

PART I

1	The Acronym SWAE	7
2	Two Major Characteristics of SWAE	15
3	Elements of SWAE: The Clause	19
4	Elements of SWAE: The Phrase	23
5	Classifying Clauses	27
6	The Flexible Clause	33
7	Verbal Phrases	37
8	Sentence Patterns	41
9	Additional Clause Patterns	45
10	The Flexible Phrase	49

PART II

11	The Big Three	55
12	Agreement I: Subjects and Verbs	65
13	Agreement II: Pronouns	75
14	Additional Pronoun Problems	81
15	Modification	91
16	Punctuation	97
17	"Form Is the Shape of Content"	103

Epilogue	107
Bibliography	111

Preface

What Is Standard Written American English (SWAE)?

When I was on vacation in Florida last winter, I was reading the local newspaper, and I came across a zoning-issue article that caught my eye. What captured my attention was this sentence: "Her's was the most important statement." I guess that I must have made a funny, strangling sound, because my wife Amy asked, "Are you okay?" to which I replied, "I can't believe the copy editor let this slip by! This is a mistake that my remedial English students make." My wife is used to outbursts like this.

As you may have guessed, I am an English teacher. More specifically, I am an English professor at Lakeland Community College in Kirtland, Ohio—or I should say, I *was* a professor. I am now retired and only occasionally teach a course or give a lecture. But I am always thinking of language and its various uses. And in my retirement I have become a writer myself, having written several books on the films of Alfred Hitchcock.

Teaching writing on the college level (it is usually referred to as "composition," a term that has always seemed to me pompous and stiff) and becoming a writer myself, I have thought for a long time that something has been missing in the way we, as teachers and writers, have approached the special kind of language that we ask our audience to read and our students to master, a word that implies a struggle for control of some sort. And struggle my students usually do! Frequently they lose the struggle and become over-mastered by a form of the very language they use in their everyday conversations.

Community colleges, because of their open-door policy, are frequently on the front lines of this language battle. Many of our students have had difficulties with the kind of English that they are expected to use in their classes, whether in English or in nursing. The social, economic, and political causes of educational inequalities in contemporary America are too broad and complex for me to address. We are all aware of the caste and class divisions in American society.

But I *can* speak to the reason why students from all castes and classes seem to have difficulty understanding and complying with the demands of written English. Simply put, written English is a special kind of English—some would call it a dialect—that is often referred to as Standard English. I should like to expand the term a bit and call it Standard Written American English, which I shall refer to from now on as SWAE.

The problem with our teaching of classes that require SWAE is that we never bother to explain what this is and why we require students to use it. Consequently, the major goal of this book is to introduce SWAE not only to students but to the general public as well in the hope that knowing the rules can help one to win the game!

Acknowledgments

I wish to thank all my students who convinced me that there was a better way to teach writing. Thanks also to Alice Simon, proofreader and graphic designer extraordinaire, and Joe Smith, Hitchcock colleague and fellow writer. And finally, a big thank you to my wife, Amy, who served as sounding board and audience/critic.

Introduction

Why Writers Have Difficulty with SWAE

The difficulties with SWAE are not limited to college students and the general public; professional writers, including journalists, are not above breaking or violating the "rules" of SWAE, as demonstrated by the newspaper article mentioned in the preface. The writer had made a very common mistake with the possessive pronoun "hers," which, unlike possessive case nouns—Nancy's, Vanessa's—does not take an apostrophe. In fact, none of the possessive pronouns ending is "s"—yours, his, hers, ours, theirs, its—take an apostrophe.

Like most errors in SWAE, the use of "her's" for "hers" is due to a misapplication of a well-known but troublesome rule about the formation of possessive nouns. When the mistake was pointed out to the writer, she was thankful, claiming that she valued careful readers of her pieces. In a letter to the editor about this common error, the writer, a published author, described some of the embarrassing errors that slipped through in the early drafts of his books. It turns out that even professional writers make errors and that writers of all kinds and abilities must submerge their egos and listen to their readers when such errors occur.

The email exchange and the letter to the editor about the journalist's error highlight an important characteristic of SWAE: there are rules governing its usage and practices, but these rules are not codified in any one "bible" of usage. In short, there is no official rulebook, as there is in, say, Major League Baseball, which has its *Official Baseball Rules*.

Perhaps things would be easier if there were such a rulebook, or if there were an official American English Language Academy, like the French l'Académie française, established in 1635. Its forty members, *les immortels* (the immortals), are elected for life. Their task is to uphold the high standards of the French language.[1] Unfortunately for American students, but fortunately for English itself, we have no government-sponsored group that rules on American English usage.

It's fortunate because one of the strengths of American English is its endless variety of forms and borrowing, its lack of a conservative body "to apply the brakes" to language change. As a result, modern English is a dynamic organism that has become a dominant force in world culture. But it's also unfortunate because the rules of SWAE seem to belong to an anointed few, who mysteriously apply rules that novice writers must learn. The journalist at the local newspaper knew the "rule" about possessive pronouns, and she understood when it was pointed out that she had violated that rule. This kind of tacit agreement is one of the things that puzzle those who are trying to learn how to use SWAE.

Even though SWAE lacks an official rulebook, it does have a variety of authoritative sources that writers can consult to get answers to questions of usage. Frequently, organizations that are involved in writing or writing instruction require their employees to use a "house" stylebook or manual. Such is the case with the Associated Press, which requires its journalists to use the *Associated Press Stylebook*, more commonly known as the *AP Stylebook*, which has been adopted by many newspapers as their official house stylebook.

At Lakeland Community College, the English Department adopted *The Little, Brown Handbook* (Fowler and Aaron) and required all English students to purchase the book. Yet, in a neighboring county, the English Department at a private university required its freshman English students to purchase *The Little Seagull Handbook* (Bullock and Weinberg), while at the same institution, the university's publications department, which was in charge of all "official" communications with the public, required its writers to adhere to the *AP Stylebook*.

Moreover, when faculty at this university published the results of their scholarly and critical research, the book and journal publishers could require writers to follow *The Chicago Manual of Style*, or *The MLA Style Manual and Guide to Scholarly Publishing*, or the *AP Stylebook*, or a myriad of other rulebooks. "Go figure" would be a legitimate response to this variety within the same institution.

Frequently, the variety takes place in a single writer's work. For example, in the author's book on Hitchcock, *Psycho in the Shower: The History of Cinema's Most Famous Scene*, the publisher required *The MLA Style Manual and Guide to Scholarly Publishing*, while in the second book, *Dark Energy: Hitchcock's Absolute Camera and the Physics of Cinematic Spacetime*, Bloomsbury Press mandated *The Chicago Manual of Style*. Each of these guides had contrasting methods for documenting sources (books, articles, interviews, etc.) and for settling questions of usage.

At this point, one might ask if it's possible to have any consistency in this seeming hodgepodge of "rules and regulations." There is, and the key lies in the email exchange with the journalist described at the beginning of this introduction. There *is* a general sense of agreement within the writing and publishing communities about what is acceptable usage and what is not. It's "general" because there are some gray areas that cause trouble and confusion.

One such area is the rule that says a pronoun should agree in number (singular or plural) with the word that the pronoun refers to, sometimes called the pronoun's antecedent. So the sentence "The captain asked that everybody on the boat wear their lifejackets" is technically incorrect, since the pronoun "everybody" is *supposedly* always singular and "their" is plural. What is meant by "supposedly" is that many established writers would stick with the original sentence since changing the antecedent to singular would raise the problem of "sexist" language: "The captain asked that everybody wear his or her lifejacket."

Many writers don't like or use the "his or her" construction (sometimes written as "his/her") since they believe it sounds awkward and wordy. Yet many writers would opt for the "his or her" in order to avoid being labeled "sexist." Some writers, however, would avoid the problem altogether by choosing a different pronoun: "The captain asked that all of the passengers wear their lifejackets."

In her delightful and erudite memoir *Between You & Me: Confessions of a Comma Queen*, Mary Norris, a copy editor at the prestigious *New Yorker* magazine, says this about the pronoun number problem: "I hate to say it, but the colloquial use of 'their' when you mean 'his or her' is just wrong. It may solve the gender problem, and there is no doubt that it has taken over in the spoken language, but it does so at the expense of number. An antecedent that is in the singular cannot take a plural pronoun. And yet it does, all the time—certainly in speech. It's not fair."[2]

It should be kept in mind that Norris is speaking of colloquial dialect, not a SWAE one. However, colloquialisms frequently creep into standard usage, as can be seen by the "everybody/their" dilemma. One recent cultural change has had an impact on pronoun usage: the rise of the lesbian, gay, bisexual, transgender, and queer community, known by the acronym LGBTQ. On the University of Wisconsin at Milwaukee's website for its Lesbian, Gay, Bisexual, Transgender Resource Center, the following suggestions have been made for inclusion of "gender neutral" pronouns:

he/she—zie
him/her—zim
his/her—zir
his/hers—zis
himself/herself—zieself[3]

SWAE almost always provides ways of solving usage problems in these gray areas, even though some writers may not consider the solution "fair." Since SWAE by its very nature is conservative, it may be quite a while before the above pronoun suggestions seep into the language. In the following chapters, the focus will be on the structure of SWAE sentences since all writing begins with sentences, strings of words arranged for meaning and style.

The great Romantic poet Samuel Taylor Coleridge's definition of poetry—"the best words in the best order"—has frequently been paraphrased for a description of prose: "the right words in the right order." That seems an apt definition of a sentence, so the next few chapters will deal with what is right about SWAE sentences.

ESSENTIAL IDEAS IN THE INTRODUCTION

- Professional writers sometimes break the rules of SWAE.
- There is no "official" rulebook for SWAE.
- There are a variety of authoritative sources.

NOTES

1. "French Academy: French Literary Organization," *Encyclopaedia Britannica*, http://www.britannica.com/topic/french-academy (accessed December 1, 2017).

2. Mary Norris, *Between You & Me: Confessions of a Comma Queen* (New York: W. W. Norton & Company, 2015), 69.

3. Lesbian, Gay, Bisexual, Transgender Resource Center, University of Wisconsin at Milwaukee, https://umw.edu/lgbtrc/support/gender-pronouns/ (accessed November 15, 2017).

PART I

One

The Acronym SWAE

In the introduction, the term SWAE was used to describe the kind of English that students are required to use in their college courses. In addition, many professional writers use SWAE, even though they may not be aware of the term. The term SWAE is an acronym, a word, usually in all capital letters, that is coined from the initial letters of related words. *The American Heritage College Dictionary* defines "acronym" in this way: "A word formed from the initial letters or parts of a word, such as *PAC* for *p*olitical *a*ction *c*ommittee."[1] Quoting a source and citing the source of the quotation are important aspects of SWAE; all handbooks and style manuals provide methods for using and then citing sources.

This is perhaps an appropriate time to discuss what is sometimes called "academic misconduct" or "plagiarism." If you are a college student, you've most likely encountered your college's student conduct policy, which covers things like cheating, plagiarizing, and general student behavior. Because SWAE has "standard" as its initial word, the concept is grounded upon adhering to a high level of integrity in presenting written material. In short, SWAE demands that you distinguish clearly between material you borrow to develop your ideas and material you have in your store of common knowledge.

You must be careful, however, in the way you apply this idea of common knowledge. This is how the Online Writing Lab (OWL) at Purdue University defines the term:

> Generally speaking, you can regard something as common knowledge if you find the same information undocumented in at least five credible sources. Additionally, it might be common knowledge if you think the information is something your readers will already know, or something that a person could easily find in general reference sources. But when in doubt, cite; if the citation turns out to be unnecessary, your teacher or editor will tell you.[2]

When teachers discuss plagiarism with their students at the beginning of the term, they usually take special care to point out that plagiarism refers not only to using the exact words of a source without acknowledging that source but also to "borrowing" ideas from a source without acknowledging that source, even though you are paraphrasing the ideas in your own words.

Writers of SWAE thus have a moral and ethical obligation to present material honestly and conscientiously. Even professional writers are held to this standard; that is why good writers have editors and fact checkers who make sure that all sources are correctly attributed and documented carefully. Throughout this book, there are models that demonstrate correct methods of incorporating material from a source and then documenting that source. There are many different methods for documentation, but they are all based on the key idea of integrity and honesty.

Now let's get back to the SWAE acronym. The first and most significant word of the acronym is "standard." *Webster's Third New International Dictionary* provides eighteen definitions of this word, the fourth of which reads: "something that is established by authority, custom or general consent as a model or example to be followed." The dictionary provides these as synonyms: "criterion," "yardstick," and "touchstone."[3]

The world-renowned language scholar David Crystal defines "standard" as "a variety of a language which has acquired special prestige within a community."[4] One of the most important authoritative sources for establishing what is standard usage is the dictionary, specifically *Webster's New International Dictionary*. The dictionary definition quoted above comes from the third edition, which was published amid great controversy in 1961.

The hubbub arose because the third edition reversed the priority of the second edition (1934), which had as one of its goal to prescribe correct usage. The third edition *described* the way the language was being used, not how it ought to be used. This question of prescriptive versus descriptive is at the very heart of the problem of authority. In a sense, *Webster's New International Dictionary* is the closest that English has to the Major League Baseball rulebook. When the 1961 edition came out, it seemed to some writers and teachers that it changed the rules of the game in a drastic way.

Of course, the question of authority is one of the thorny issues in SWAE. As part of the research for this book, an informal survey was sent to ten friends and acquaintances of the author, who were involved in one way or another with writing. One of the questions asked whether the recipients had ever heard of the acronyms SWAE or SWE (Standard Written English). Almost all said that they had not. There was no surprise in this result.

Other questions asked about sources of authority for usage questions, and several recipients answered that published writers—that is, those writers of fiction and nonfiction whose works are published in reputable newspapers, journals, and books—are the most reliable sources of authority. Other survey recipients mentioned the various guidebooks and style manuals mentioned in the introduction, as well as the numerous dictionaries that are available, both in print and online.

The major point is that there is no singular "gold standard" but rather many sources of authority. Perhaps *Webster's Third* can help answer the question "Who makes the rules?" The dictionary defines the term "Standard English" as "the writing of the educated," and that seems a good benchmark to use. Thus, an educated writer would not produce a sentence like: "The actor realized that he should not have went to the movie's premiere" since the verb "should have went" is nonstandard, "gone" being the correct past participle of the verb "to go." This is the standard sentence: "The actor realized that he should not have gone to the movie's premiere."

The second word of our acronym, "written," seems self-evident, but it really isn't. Written English and spoken English are related, but they are not the same. The differences cause dissension not only in the ranks of English teachers but also among those who use English professionally. As noted above, this kind of conflict surfaced dramatically in 1961 with the publication of *Webster's Third New International Dictionary*, the purpose of which was to describe how the language was being used, not necessarily how it should be used.

This purpose was evidence of a new orientation to the English language championed by linguists, those who study English "scientifically." On the whole, linguists are more interested in spoken English than in written English. To a linguist, all dialects of English are equal. There is no one dialect that is better or more preferable than another.

Of course, this attitude seems to fly in the face of SWAE, which has at its core the idea of standard versus nonstandard usage. In short, SWAE mandates that one grammatical form—"should have gone"—is more correct than another form—"should have went." However, the term "more correct" must be seen in the context of the SWAE dialect. In the context of colloquial English dialect—informal, spoken English—the verb "should have went" (sometimes pronounced as if it's spelled "should of went") is often acceptable, even among educated users who sometimes slip into this usage without even realizing it.

A vivid example of the linguistic approach to language is Yale University's Grammatical Diversity Project, under the leadership of Professor Raffaella Zanuttini of the Linguistics Department. The project, according to Peggy Edersheim Kalb, who wrote about it for the *Yale Alumni Magazine*, "is compiling existing data on the grammar of many varieties of American English. . . . Their goal: to create a repository for all the research done to date on the varieties of English they're investigating."

What is fascinating about this project is that its focus is on the grammar (rules and regulations governing the structure of sentences) and not just on regional accents and vocabularies. For example, the project recorded these sentences, which would be considered nonstandard in SWAE: "Are you done your ice?" and "Here's you a spoon."

The project's approach to English, according to the article's author, is nondiscriminatory; in other words, no one dialect is better than the other. All the recorded expressions are understood by the people who share that particular dialect. Kalb states, "In much of the Midwest, 'anymore' can mean 'these days'—in an affirmative sentence, as in 'Those are worthless anymore.'"[5]

The Grammatical Diversity Project is a perfect example of the descriptive approach to English, which is the basis for linguistics. The project collects data and studies it in a scientific manner, avoiding any kind of prejudice. It's telling that the Linguistics Department at Yale is separate from the English Department, signifying a different and sometimes adversarial approach to language.

However, as pointed out above, SWAE is prescriptive; the word "standard" means that there is a yardstick or a criterion by which written sentences are measured (i.e., "the right words in the right order"). In the paragraphs above, it was claimed that SWAE could be considered a dialect of English, so it is fitting to define the word "dialect" as it pertains to English.

Webster's Third New International Dictionary has several definitions of the word. Linguists would use the first definition: "a variety of language that is used by one group of persons and has features of vocabulary, grammar, or pronunciation distinguishing it from other varieties used by other groups." Thus, a dialect is a means by which language groups are separated from one another. No one dialect is superior to another.

However, there is another definition of "dialect" that is more appropriate for SWAE: "a manner or means of expressing oneself especially in language."[6] In an important sense, SWAE is a dialect of English that unites people rather than separates them. No matter what linguistic dialect one speaks, one can learn SWAE and communicate with other SWAE writers. In essence, then, SWAE is the most democratic dialect, since it makes all people equal and unites them in a common method of written language. David Crystal states:

> The role of a standard language, whether it is used nationally or internationally, is to enable the members of a community to understand each other. Everyone needs to learn it, in the interests of efficient and effective communication. This is why in school we are taught to read and write Standard English, and are given opportunities to read it aloud and to hear others read it. The leading national institutions, such as the British Parliament, the US

Congress, the BBC, and CNN, adopt it as their primary means of expression, in the interests of universal comprehensibility, so we hear it widely spoken in public as the language of power and prestige. Its expressive potential is exploited throughout English literature. It has an especially high profile among foreign learners of English.[7]

The third word of the acronym, "American," seems almost too obvious to explain. It is true that American English derives from British English since the original colonies were under British rule. However, American English began to be distinguished from British English with the publication in 1828 of Noah Webster's monumental *American Dictionary of the English Language*. This dictionary, along with Webster's earlier publication on American spelling, established a truly American form of English.

According to the Merriam-Webster website, Webster "believed fervently in the developing cultural independence of the United States, a chief part of which was to be a distinctive American language with its own idiom, pronunciation, and style."[8] Approximately one hundred years later, H. L. Mencken published his monumental *American Language* (1921), which claimed to look at the differences between British English and American English in a dispassionate and scientific manner.

Considering Webster's and Mencken's accomplishments, SWAE can be seen as a key component of American culture. Even though British and American writers and speakers can usually understand each other, there are some fundamental differences between the two dialects of English. Perhaps the most famous statement about British and American English is attributed to George Bernard Shaw: "England and America are two countries separated by a common language."

When commentators like Shaw discuss the differences between the two languages, they are usually referring to the spoken forms of English. In British society, social class is more defining of a person than it is in American society. In fact, the phrase "branded on the tongue" refers to the social stigma associated with the speech of "lower" classes of society. According to the British newspaper *The Independent*, Britain has seven social classes, each one determined by wealth, occupation, and education, the last of which is indicated by the type of dialect spoken.[9]

In fact, even though Britain has no "official" dialect, that of London and East Midlands is the language of law, literature, and education. The scholar who studies the function of language in society is called a "sociolinguist."

There are several significant differences between the written forms of British and American English, mainly in spelling, punctuation, and subject-verb relationship. These differences will be dealt with in later chapters.

The last word of the acronym, "English," is the anchor word, for it defines and qualifies the three words that precede and modify it. American English has become an international language, much as French was in the nineteenth century. American English reflects the power and importance of the United States in world affairs. The United States did not invent the language: it was "inherited," in a sense, from the British when they colonized the North American continent. And, of course, Great Britain spread English around the world in the nineteenth and early twentieth centuries while building the British Empire.

Like other languages, English has evolved over the centuries and has been subject to changes and modifications along the way. In fact, one fascinating new field in sociolinguistics is called "World Englishes." No, that last word is not a typo. The field of "World Englishes" involves an examination of the many varieties of English spoken around the world. The major emphasis is on spoken English, but the written form is also studied for its hybrid character.

An instance of World English was discussed at a class at Lakeland Community College. Augustine, an international student, was from Liberia, where the English that is spoken is called "Broken English," and it is a hybrid of English and African tribal dialects. The students, as well as the professor, were fascinated to hear how Broken English blended dialects in a creative way.

The English language evolved from a parent language, what linguists call Indo-European. This "proto" language gave birth to many offspring. The important point here is that language changes, unless it is a "dead" language like Latin. In fact, at present, the language is changing and shifting, just as the tectonic plates beneath the earth's surface are constantly shifting and rubbing against one another. The key is to understand that written English, in particular SWAE, changes more slowly than spoken English. In essence, written English is more "standard" than spoken.

In many coffee-shop conversations, one hears customers claim that they are horrified by the construction "should of went" (phonetically, "of" is really a shortening of "have"). But paradoxically, they don't object to "It's me," which is incorrect, according to SWAE, since the verb "to be" does not take objects. Not many people, even well-educated ones, would say, "It's I."

The hard fact here is that one is judged by the language one uses, especially written language. Any student who has taken an English class knows that the assigned "papers" frequently come back with many corrections. In the special situation of the classroom, there *is* a recognized and legitimate authority of SWAE: the teacher or professor.

ESSENTIAL IDEAS IN THIS CHAPTER

- SWAE is an acronym.
- In SWAE, all sources must be documented.
- Plagiarism is a serious violation of academic honesty.
- The "standard" in the acronym means a criterion or yardstick.
- Written English has different standards than spoken English.
- SWAE changes more slowly than spoken English.

NOTES

1. *American Heritage College Dictionary* (Boston: Houghton Mifflin Company, 1993), 12.
2. Purdue Online Writing Lab (OWL), https://owl.english.purdue.edu/owl/resource/589/02 (accessed November 16, 2017).
3. *Webster's Third New International Dictionary of the English Language Unabridged* (Springfield, MA: G and C Merriam Company, 1961), 2223.
4. David Crystal, *The Stories of English* (Woodstock NY: Overlook Press, 2004), 6.
5. Peggy Kalb, "Why 'Bad' English Isn't," *Yale Alumni Magazine*, July/August 2013, https://yalealumnimagazine.com/articles/3716.
6. See *Webster's Third New International Dictionary of the English Language Unabridged*, 622–632.
7. Crystal, *The Stories of English*, 6.
8. "Noah Webster and America's First Dictionary," Merriam-Webster, https://www.merriam-webster.com/info/noah.htm (accessed September 2017).
9. Laura Davis, "Britain's 7 new social classes: do you fit into one?" *Independent*, April 3, 2013. https://www.independent.co.uk/voices/iv-drip/britains-7-new-social-classes-do-you-fit-into-one-8558145.html.

Two

Two Major Characteristics of SWAE

Now that a definition of SWAE has been established, it is important to examine in detail the two major characteristics of this dialect. However, it would be helpful at this point to reiterate the major points made in the previous chapter and the introduction.

1. SWAE is a dialect of English that has its own "rules" and "regulations," but SWAE does not have a definitive rulebook.
2. Written language and spoken language are related to one another, but they are not the same.
3. Spoken language changes more rapidly than written language does.
4. SWAE is a "universal" dialect in that it can be understood and utilized by people no matter what dialect of English they speak.
5. SWAE is the dialect of educated people.

The two key characteristics of SWAE are connected to one another. The first is that SWAE is conservative; the second is that it is rule-bound. Each of these is important in understanding the special quality of this dialect. The term "conservative" does not relate to politics, although a political conservative would understand why SWAE has this characteristic. Both political conservatives and users of SWAE are resistant to change; both look to the past for models of correctness.

With SWAE, it is just as Tevye sings in *Fiddler on the Roof*: "Tradition, tradition!" It is this conservative, traditional characteristic that makes it possible for readers to understand a passage from a book published 134 years ago. Here, for example, is an excerpt from the opening paragraph of Henry James's *Portrait of a Lady* (1881):

> Under certain circumstances there are few hours in life more agreeable than the hour dedicated to the ceremony known as afternoon tea. There are circumstances in which, whether you partake of the tea or not—some people of course never do—the situation is in itself delightful. Those that I have in mind in beginning to unfold this simple history offered an admirable setting

to an innocent pastime. The implements of the little feast had been disposed upon the lawn of an old English country-house in what I should call the perfect middle of a splendid summer afternoon.[1]

Compare this to Mark Twain's masterful rendering of the slave Jim's dialect in *The Adventures of Huckleberry Finn*, published at about the same time as James's novel: "Yo' ole father doan' know yit what he's a-gwyne to do. Sometimes he spec he'll go way, en den agin he spec he'll stay. De bes' way is to res' easy en let de ole man mak' his own way."[2]

In attempting to capture the particular flavor of Jim's dialect, Twain demonstrates that spoken language is subject to the whims of the individual speaker, who doesn't necessarily adhere to a standard form. James's language, on the other hand, shows that the standards the novelist adhered to over a century ago are not very different from the ones a writer of SWAE would employ today.

Until the advent of graduate-level rhetoric and composition programs, many college teachers of English were not taught how to teach their students to write. They just taught writing the way they were taught by their college English teachers. Students were assigned "papers" to write on various topics. It was assumed that students knew what a "paper" was and why they were expected to write one.

Moreover, most students were never told why English was a required course for all college students. So, in a sense, the teaching of English was a conservative enterprise, and thus looking to the past and following established guidelines went hand in hand with the conservative nature of SWAE. Tradition!

The second major characteristic of SWAE is that it is rule-bound, but paradoxically there is no definitive rulebook where one can find all the rules. Now is perhaps the best time to discuss that dreaded word "grammar." The Merriam-Webster online dictionary defines grammar as "the set of rules that explain how words are used in a language."[3]

For example, the statement "Because the student did not study for the test. She flunked the course" violates a basic grammatical "rule" about sentence fragments. The word group beginning with "because" is a fragment since it lacks a main clause and is thus not a "complete sentence." The terms that describe the rule about sentence fragments are part of the grammar of SWAE.

Linguists have their own grammar terminology, which is not always the same as that employed by teachers and users of SWAE. Linguists employ grammatical terminology to *describe* the way a language works, while teachers of SWAE use grammar terms not only to describe but also to *prescribe* how the language should work. The tension between the two language orientations arises from the fact that linguists are more interested in spoken language than in written language.

The following chapters are thus partly about grammar but also about a dialect of English that employs grammar in a particular way. It is true that many readers enjoy discussions of grammar in books like Lynne Truss's delightful *Eats, Shoots & Leaves* or Mignon Fogarty's *Grammar Girl* series. So an important part of this book is about grammar. However, SWAE is more than what is wrong with sentences—what violates the "rules"—but more so what is right about sentences—what makes them work.

ESSENTIAL IDEAS IN THIS CHAPTER

- SWAE is the dialect of educated people.
- SWAE is conservative.
- SWAE resists change.
- Many teachers fail to explain to their students why English is a required course.

NOTES

1. Henry James, *Portrait of a Lady* (New York: Macmillan and Co. Ltd., 1881), 1.
2. Mark Twain, *The Adventures of Huckleberry Finn* (New York: Chatto and Windus, 1885), 10.
3. https://www.merriam-webster.com (accessed November 12, 2017).

Three

Elements of SWAE

The Clause

How do SWAE sentences work? What are their component parts, and how do these parts work together? These are the questions that will be dealt with in the next few chapters. The most important part of a SWAE sentence is the clause, which is a group of related words with a subject-verb relationship. The first part of the definition—"a group of related words"—is important in understanding what a clause is. The word group "house front in of place took accident the my" is not made up of *related* words. If the words are rearranged, we have the clause "The accident took place in front of my house."

The second part of the definition—"with a subject-verb relationship"—is really the heart of the definition: without a subject and verb, there is no clause. The verb is the essence of a clause and also its most important and complex part. A verb can be made up of one word—for example, "went"—or more than one word—"should have gone." The verb can show action—"I ran a marathon"—or it can show a state of being—"I was very tired."

Once you've found the verb, you can find the subject by asking, "Who or what ran or was tired?" The answer in both cases is "I." Take the clause "Roberto should have taken the test." First find the verb, and then the subject. If you said the verb is "should have taken" and the subject is "Roberto," you would be correct.

There are two types of clauses, main and subordinate. If you've studied clauses before, you might have learned a slightly different terminology for the two types of clauses: independent and dependent. It really makes no difference which terms you choose, as long as you don't mix the terminology—"main" and "dependent," for example—since that can lead to confusion. "Main" and "subordinate" are preferable only because the two words are different enough that they don't get confused. In addition, many students insist on spelling "independent" as "independ*a*nt"!

The main clause is the key element of SWAE sentences. Without a main clause, a sentence is not a sentence—in SWAE terms, that is. However, even professional writers violate this crucial criterion. For example, John Baxter's wonderful book *A Pound of Paper* contains the following passage:

> Collecting a writer's work is a way of owning the artist you admire, and each step in the collection of a title takes you closer to the author. First, a copy of the book, perhaps a paperback, just to read. Then, once you decide you like it, a more durable edition. After that, the first edition, followed by a first with the author's signature. Then the proof copy, which precedes the first printing. Then the manuscript.[1]

If you were asked to identify the fragments in the above passage, which word groups would you choose? Of the six word groups, only the first is a "legitimate" sentence in SWAE terms. The other five word groups are fragments. It's true some of the word groups contain subject-verb relationships—"once you decide you like it," for example—but these are not main clauses.

At this point, it would be helpful to define a main clause, as it will be used for the remainder of this book: *a main clause is a group of related words with a subject-verb relationship that can stand alone as a sentence.* The budding logicians out there might fault this definition as a tautology, a kind of circular definition. But as you shall see, this definition works for the purpose of this book.

If all clauses contain subject-verb relationships, then what distinguishes a main from a subordinate clause? The answer is in the word or words that introduce the clause, what will be called a clause marker. Just as with "main" and "independent," there are different terms for the word or sometimes words that introduce a clause: subordinating conjunction, relative pronoun, subordinating word(s). These are all terms that refer to clause markers.

It is important to keep in mind that terminology should not be confused with the thing itself. The terminology of SWAE is simply a way to label things in order to talk about them. For example, in grammar terminology, the word "train" can be called a noun, or, in the sentence "The train pulled out of the station," it can be called a subject. The word has two terms to describe it, and both are correct.

Thus, in the sentence "The train pulled out of the station when all the passengers had been boarded," there are two clauses: the first is the sentence looked at earlier, "The train pulled out of the station." It is a main clause because it can stand by itself as a sentence. The second clause, "when all the passengers had been boarded," is a subordinate clause because of the word "when," which is a clause marker. So the sentence has two clauses, which can be symbolized thus: MC SC.

It's possible to remove the clause marker and state the same ideas with two main clauses. "The passengers had all been boarded. The train pulled out of the station." The sentences would be symbolized in this way: MC. MC. As long as you have a main clause, you have the basis of a sentence. What is not considered correct in SWAE is stating the ideas in this way: "The train pulled out of the station. When the passengers had all been boarded." The second word group, although it has a subject-verb relationship, is not a sentence because it lacks a main clause.

As will be discussed, many writers use fragments as a stylistic device, as in the excerpt from John Baxter's book above. But when you're first learning about SWAE, it is important to follow the rules whenever you can. So here is Cardinal Rule #1: *All SWAE sentences must contain at least one main clause.*

As practice, can you identify main clauses in the sentences below? Which of the italicized clauses are main clauses?

1. *Whenever I take a cruise*, I always feel seasick on the first day.
2. *I just bought a new car*, which cost quite a bit of money.
3. I just bought a new car, *and it cost quite a bit of money*.
4. *Although Juan studied hard for the test*, he did not pass it.
5. Juan studied hard for the test, *but he did not pass it*.

If you answered 2, 3, and 5, you are correct. Numbers 1 and 4 are subordinate clauses because of the clause markers "whenever" and "although."

If you thought that 3 and 5 were subordinate clauses, you've made a very common mistake with the words "and" and "but," which are not clause markers but rather "coordinating conjunctions." These are words that can connect clauses but do not turn them into subordinate clauses.

This misidentification is unfortunately caused by many well-intentioned language arts teachers, who tell their students never to start sentences with "and" or "but." Actually, sentences 3 and 5 could be rewritten in the following ways and still be correct: "I just bought a new car. And it cost quite a bit of money." "Juan studied hard for the test. But he did not pass it." There's much more to learn about clauses, as the upcoming chapters will demonstrate.

ESSENTIAL IDEAS IN THIS CHAPTER

- A clause is a group of related words with a subject-verb relationship.
- There are two types of clauses: main and subordinate.
- The main clause is the key element of SWAE sentences.

- A subordinate clause is introduced by a clause marker and cannot stand alone as a SWAE sentence.
- Cardinal Rule #1 is that all SWAE sentences must contain at least one main clause.

NOTE

1. John Baxter, *A Pound of Paper: Confessions of a Book Addict* (New York: Thomas Dunne Books, St. Martin's Press, 2002), 4–5.

Four

Elements of SWAE

The Phrase

See if you can find the clauses in the following word groups:

1. Between the two teams
2. Roberto, our new boss
3. Must have been talking
4. Running my first marathon
5. Buried in the backyard
6. To start my own business

If you were unable to find a clause in any of the word groups, then you're beginning to understand the concept. As you were searching for clauses, you might have noticed that all of the above are made up of related words but have no subject-verb relationships. So what is a group of related words that does *not* have a subject-verb relationship called? This is called a phrase. All six of the above word groups are phrases of different types.

1. prepositional phrase: a preposition—in this case, "between"—and an object, which is the last word in the phrase—in this case, "teams."
2. appositive phrase: a noun or pronoun that renames a noun or pronoun that precedes or follows it. In this word group, "our new boss" renames "Roberto." Most appositives are set off by commas.
3. verb phrase: a verb that is made up of auxiliary (or "helping") verbs and a main verb, which is usually the last word in the phrase. In this case, "must," "have," and "been" are auxiliaries, and "talking" is the main verb.
4. gerund phrase: an –ing phrase used as a noun.
5. past participial phrase, present participial phrase: a word group functioning as an adjective. The present participial phrase looks exactly like a gerund phrase. What distinguishes them is how they are used. The past participial phrase can take different forms, depending on the form of the past participle of the verb. Here are some

examples: "The concoction *drunk by the robbers* rendered them unconscious. The action *carried out by the committee* alienated the workers."
6. infinitive phrase: the word "to" plus a verb and its modifiers or objects.

What would happen if main clauses were added to each of these phrases?

1. The coach noticed the animosity between the two teams.
2. Roberto, our new boss, made some changes to our work schedules.
3. Joan's cousin must have been talking behind her back.
4. Running my first marathon was extremely difficult.
5. The bone buried in the backyard was discovered by my dog, Maisie.
6. I wanted to start my own business.

Can you see what happened to the phrases? They became parts of SWAE sentences. That is, they now all have main clauses and thus satisfy Cardinal Rule #1: All SWAE sentences must have at least one main clause.

Phrases raise interesting problems for those using SWAE. In order to explore these problems, you must return to grammar, the set of rules for sentence construction. Many of you probably were introduced to grammar through the "parts-of-speech" approach, which establishes eight categories: nouns, verbs, adjectives, adverbs, pronouns, prepositions, conjunctions, and interjections (actually nine, if you count articles).

This traditional approach to grammar, though, is only part of how words actually function in sentences. In addition, the word "speech" can be confusing when discussing written English. A functional level of grammar therefore needs to be added to the categories—words or word groups that function as subjects, objects, and modifiers.

For example, the single word "race" can be a subject: "The race begins at noon"; an object: "He entered the race"; a verb: "We race every Saturday"; an adjective: "Today is race day"; and an object of a preposition: "Jack went to the race." In addition, "race" can become a verbal, a word derived from a verb but not functioning as a verb in a clause. "Racing can be a rewarding hobby." In this sentence, "racing" is functioning both as a noun and a subject. "I gave racing a try." In this sentence, "racing" is functioning both as a noun and an object. "He had a passion for racing." In this sentence, "racing" is both a noun and an object of a preposition. The function of a word like "race," then, depends upon its position in the sentence—its word order.

Moving from single words to phrases, one encounters problems with word functions based on placement. Linguists call English an "analytical language" because it has lost many of the inflectional endings that identify a word as a subject, object, and so on, regardless of its position in a sentence.

Elements of SWAE

English developed from a prototype language called Indo-European, which had many inflectional endings to identify the function of a word.

Latin, for example, also traces its origins to the Indo-European source language. But Latin is highly inflectional. The function of a word depends on its form and endings, not on its position in the sentence. The noun *agricola* (farmer), for instance, has these forms:

Nominative: (subject) agricola = **The farmer** grew the wheat.
Genitive: (possessive) agricolae = This is the home **of the farmer**.
Dative: (indirect object) agricolae = He gave **the farmer** some wheat.
Accusative: (direct object) agricolam = He sued **the farmer**.
Ablative: (object of preposition) agricola = He talked **with the farmer**.

The verbal phrase "running a marathon" is an example of what can happen to phrases as they are used in SWAE. There's no way of telling by the phrase itself whether it is functioning as a noun subject, a noun object, a noun object of a preposition, or an adjective.

1. **Running a marathon** is a grueling activity. Noun subject.
2. I tried **running a marathon**. Noun object.
3. I set aside time for **running a marathon**. Noun object of preposition.
4. **Running a marathon**, Jim injured his leg. Adjective modifying "Jim."

Moreover, phrases—and clauses as well—can be embedded. That is, phrases can be contained within phrases. In sentence 3 above, the verbal phrase "running a marathon" is part of the prepositional phrase "for running a marathon." Sometimes phrases can be within phrases that are within phrases—like looking at a reflection in a mirror reflected in a mirror. Take the sentence "Running for the bus in the morning can be a frustrating experience." The subject of the sentence is the long verbal phrase "Running for the bus in the morning"; that phrase is actually three phrases: the verbal phrase, and then two prepositional phrases embedded in it—"for the bus" and "in the morning."

In analyzing SWAE sentences, it is important to distinguish between clauses and phrases since a phrase—no matter how long or embedded—can't stand by itself as a sentence. "Running for the bus in the morning and getting soaked by the rain" may look like a sentence, but it lacks a main clause and is thus a fragment, a major error in SWAE. This error could be fixed by connecting this word group to a main clause: "Running for the bus in the morning and getting soaked by the rain, I arrived at work in a bad mood."

Of course, the error could be corrected by converting the verbals "running" and "getting" into verbs: "ran" and "got." Here is the correction:

"I ran for the bus in the morning and got soaked by the rain. I thus arrived at work in a bad mood." Cardinal Rule #2, then, is this: *Phrases by themselves, no matter how long, cannot be considered SWAE sentences.*

As will be seen in a forthcoming chapter, putting a phrase in the "wrong" part of a sentence can lead to errors in SWAE.

ESSENTIAL IDEAS IN THIS CHAPTER

- A phrase is a group of related words without a subject-verb relationship.
- There are six types of phrases: prepositional, appositive, verb, gerund, past participial and present participial, and infinitive.
- The "parts-of-speech" grammar is the traditional approach to sentence structure.
- However, there is also a need for a different level of grammar: the functional.
- English is an analytical language.
- Cardinal Rule #2 is that phrases, by themselves, cannot be SWAE sentences, no matter how long.

Five

Classifying Clauses

As previously stated, the clause is the major building block of a sentence. And of course the main clause is the *key* component of sentences, as stated in Cardinal Rule #1: *All SWAE sentences must contain at least one main clause.* All clauses, whether subordinate or main, contain a subject-verb relationship.

The verb is the anchor of a clause and its most complex part. It can show time (tense) and number (singular or plural), but it also links the subject to other parts of the sentence. A single-word verb, such as "run," can show past action by changing a single letter—"u"—to "a": hence, "ran."

The verb can also add an "s" in the present tense to match a singular subject in a sentence like this: "The boy runs." Or the verb can drop the "s" to match a plural subject, as in this sentence: "The boys run." These are examples of inflectional endings, which are still active in certain verbs and pronouns. The verb can also connect a subject with an object: "I passed the test." Or it can connect a subject with a word that renames it or describes it: "The professor is my cousin," "The professor is brilliant."

Verbs can also be verb phrases, one of the six types of phrases discussed in chapter 4. Verb phrases are made up of auxiliary (or helping) verbs and a main verb, which is the last word in the phrase. A legendary English teacher named Miss Robbins taught eighth grade at Williams School in Chelsea, Massachusetts, during the 1940s and 1950s, when the teaching of grammar was part of the curriculum. She made all her students memorize the "verb table." To this day, students recall vividly having to stand and recite the verb table:

be, am,
is, are,
was, were,
shall, will, been,
could, would, should,
have, has, had,

do, did, does,
may, can, must,
might.

Little did her students know that Miss Robbins was giving them the tools to build any verb phrase. All that is needed is the main verb. Here are some examples:

Alfred Hitchcock **should have won** an Academy Award for Best Director.
Gerry **must have been contemplating** another run for mayor.
My aunt's friend **might have seen** a flying saucer.
I **could have been** a contender.

Clauses can be classified by the type and function of the main verb, which can be a single word or the last word in a verb phrase. One way to classify verbs is to divide them into transitive and intransitive. Both of these verb types show an action of some kind or another. A transitive verb is one that can answer the question "What?" or "Whom?" For example, in the sentence "Frances gave food to the homeless man," the verb "gave" is transitive, since we can answer the question "Gave what?" with the noun "food."

Transitive verbs can take direct objects (these objects answer the question "What or whom?") and indirect objects ("To or for what or whom?"). Usually, an indirect object is coupled with a direct object, as in the sentence "Frances gave the homeless man food." The indirect object is "homeless man," and the direct object is "food."

There is a third type of transitive verb sentence that is a variation of the direct object structure. This type of sentence has an object complement, an adjective that modifies the direct object and follows it. For example, the clause "My Uncle Lawrence painted his car blue" contains both a direct object, "car," and an object complement, "blue." Thus the first three clause classifications are the following patterns, all based on transitive verbs:

1. subject–transitive verb–direct object
2. subject–transitive verb–indirect object–direct object
3. subject–transitive verb–direct object–object complement

Intransitive verbs, on the other hand, do not take objects, but they do show action, just like the transitive verbs. Here are examples of clauses with intransitive verbs:

Jennifer fainted on her wedding day
Since Lenny sneezed in the allergy clinic
Juanita ran in the rain

The above clauses have prepositional phrases, but these phrases are not considered complements. Rather, they are functioning as adverbs, answering the questions "Where or when?" Adverbs can also answer other questions in relationship to the verb in the sentence: "To what extent?" "How many times?" "In what manner?"

The intransitive can be added to the list of clause patterns:

4. subject–intransitive verb

Transitive and intransitive verbs are classified as action verbs. There is, however, another category of verbs that is sometimes referred to as "copulative," from the Latin word for "linking." Copulative verbs express a state of being or becoming, not a state of action, although the distinction between the two is sometimes subtle. Linguists and grammarians divide copulative verbs into two categories: "to be" verbs and linking verbs. The first category—"to be" verbs—comprises various forms of the verb "to be": be, am, is, are, was, were, shall, will, and been.

In dealing with a verb phrase rather than a single-word verb, the classification of the verb is based on the main verb, the last word in the phrase. Thus, the clause "The architect is designing a new building" does not contain a "to be" verb; rather, the main verb is "designing," an action verb. The verb "is" functions as an auxiliary verb. The clause is therefore an example of pattern number one: subject–transitive verb–direct object.

Most "to be" verbs link the subject with a word that renames it or describes it. However, it's possible to have a "to be" verb in a clause like this: "I am." The famous statement from philosopher René Descartes, "I think; therefore I am," is made up of two clauses: "I think," which is the subject–intransitive verb pattern; and "therefore I am," which is the subject–"to be" verb pattern.

5. subject–"to be" verb

The next two patterns are based on the "to be" verb. An example of the first is a sentence such as "Daniel Miller is an English professor." In this sentence, the verb "is" joins the subject—Daniel Miller—with a noun (or pronoun) that renames it—English professor. The order of the sentence can be reversed: "The English professor is Daniel Miller." The pattern is the same. The noun or pronoun that renames a subject is called the "predicate nominative," a fancy term that simply means that a word (or words) that renames the subject is located in the predicate—or verb—part of the sentence.

The next pattern features a subject and a "to be" verb, but the word that appears in the predicate part of the sentence is an adjective: a "predicate adjective." The following clauses are examples of this pattern: "The new student is brilliant. The test was difficult. If the client is poor."

6. Subject–"to be" verb–predicate nominative
7. Subject–"to be" verb–predicate adjective

The final two clause patterns are similar to the previous two, but the verb is classified as a linking verb. In effect, the verb links the subject with a word that renames it or that describes it. Common linking verbs are the following: "appear," "become," "feel," "get," "grow," "look," "prove," "remain," "seem," "stay," "sound," "taste," "turn."

It's crucial to understand the difference between a verb that is expressing an action and a verb that is expressing a state of being or becoming. For example, the clause "when she smelled the flowers" is different from the clause "because the flowers smelled good," just as the clause "the chef tasted the soup" is different from the clause "the chef's soup tasted delicious."

Here are a few more examples of clauses that contain linking verbs, combined with clauses that contain action verbs:

the weather turned warm; the attendant turned the key
when Oscar became sick; the dress became her
the orchestra sounded superb; the taxi driver sounded his horn

The second example in each of the pairs above is this pattern: subject–transitive verb–direct object. The difference between transitive and linking verbs is subtle in the above examples, but with practice, one can start to see the difference. Here is an example: "The material feels smooth; Bob felt the smooth material." In the first clause, the material is not feeling anything, but in the second, Bob is performing an action: he is feeling the material.

So here are the last two clause patterns:

8. subject–linking verb–predicate nominative
9. subject–linking verb–predicate adjective

As will be seen in forthcoming chapters, the nine clause patterns above account for all the possibilities of clause constructions in SWAE. What makes language fascinating is that one can write a clause from the patterns above that has never been written before. The sentence doesn't necessarily have to make logical sense, as long as it's correctly constructed. Here, for example, is a totally original clause: "When the two pink giraffes finished their SWAE manuscript."

What is the clause pattern? The answer is "subject–transitive verb–direct object." In effect, the shifting relationships between parts-of-speech grammar and functional grammar allow SWAE writers unlimited flexibility.

ESSENTIAL IDEAS IN THIS CHAPTER

- The verb is the anchor of a clause and its most complex part.
- A verb phrase is made up of an auxiliary—or helping—verb and a main verb, which is the last word in the phrase.
- Miss Robbins's verb table contains all of the auxiliary verbs.
- Clauses are classified by the type and function of the main verb.
- A transitive verb takes an object.
- There are three transitive verb clause patterns.
- Intransitive verbs do not take objects.
- There is one intransitive verb clause pattern.
- There are three "to be" verb clause patterns.
- There are two linking verb clause patterns.

Six

The Flexible Clause

Grammatical flexibility—and knowledge—can help writers construct clauses with parts of speech and functional elements. One of the major parts of speech is the noun. Its definition is well known: a noun names a person, place, or thing. Thus, in the clause "Bob is a father," we have two nouns, "Bob" and "father." Were you able to identify the clause pattern? If you said "subject–'to be' verb–predicate nominative," you would be correct. In functional grammar, "Bob" is the subject of the above clause.

At this point, a review of a few definitions from the previous chapters is necessary to understand the structure of SWAE sentences. To reiterate, the clause is the major element in SWAE sentences, and the main clause is the key to writing "correct" SWAE sentences. It's important to remember that a clause is a group of related words with a subject-verb relationship.

In addition to the main clause, there is the subordinate clause. What's fascinating about Standard Written American English is the flexibility of the various elements that make up a sentence. The subordinate clause can actually function as three different parts of speech: noun, adjective, adverb. In effect, the subordinate clause "disguises" itself as a part of speech.

In the above sentence—"Bob is a father"—one can substitute a clause for the subject: "What I want to be is a father." This is the same sentence pattern—subject–"to be" verb–predicate nominative; but now the subject is a clause—a noun clause, because nouns can function as subjects. We can reverse the sentence so that the clause is a predicate nominative: "A father is what I want to be."

The sentences in the previous paragraph show the subordinate clause as subject and predicate nominative. However, the noun clause can also be an object—direct, indirect, or object of preposition. Let's take the two object sentence patterns and substitute noun clauses for nouns:

1. subject–transitive verb–direct object: "Roberto took the test. Roberto took whatever test was required."

2. subject–transitive verb–indirect object–direct object: "Abdul gave his friend a piece of birthday cake. Roberto gave whoever wanted it a piece of birthday cake."

A noun clause can also be part of a prepositional phrase, substituting for the object of the preposition: "Abdul gave birthday cake to his friend." "Abdul gave cake to whoever wanted a piece." In this sentence, the noun clause becomes the object of the preposition in the prepositional phrase, which has this structure: preposition + object.

As stated previously, subordinate clauses "disguise" themselves as parts of speech. This disguise is essential in resolving what seems to be a paradox in the definition of a phrase. The "phrase paradox" can cause some confusion for novice SWAE writers.

In previous paragraphs a phrase is defined as a group of related words without a subject-verb relationship. For example, in the sentence "The prize should go to the fastest runner," there is a prepositional phrase—"to the fastest runner"—that seems to fit the definition perfectly. However, if one substitutes a subordinate clause for the object of the preposition—"runner"—the sentence reads this way: "The prize should go to whoever has the fastest time."

Here is the paradox: If a prepositional phrase is a group of related words that does *not* have a subject-verb relationship, how can one explain the clause "whoever has the fastest time," which has a subject-verb relationship? The key to the paradox is the word "disguise," for the clause is "dressed up" as a noun and is functioning as the object of the preposition "to."

In order to resolve this paradox, then, one must not recognize the subordinate clause as a clause but rather believe it as a good old noun. Or, in more sophisticated terms, one is engaging in a "willing suspension of disbelief," the Romantic poet Samuel Taylor Coleridge's term for the process of believing that the play, poem, or novel is real, not make-believe.

In the discussion of phrases in chapter 4, "embedding" was defined as the process of enclosing phrases within phrases. Embedding also occurs within clauses. In the phrase discussed above—"to whoever has the fastest time"—the subordinate clause is embedded in the prepositional phrase. Sometimes the subordinate clause can function as the subject of the main clause: "Whoever has the fastest time will win the race." Can you see the clause within the clause?

Here's a more challenging question: Can you identify the clause patterns? The pattern of the main clause—actually the whole sentence—is subject–transitive verb–direct object. The pattern of the embedded clause is also subject–transitive verb–direct object. In order to sort out the various elements of a SWAE sentence, it's helpful to segment the elements by using brackets and parentheses. Brackets are used to identify clauses and parentheses to identify phrases.

Here is the above sentence segmented: [[Whoever has the fastest time] (will win) the race.] There are double brackets in front of "Whoever" because it is not only the clause marker for the subordinate clause but also the first word in the clause that functions as the subject of the main clause. There are parentheses around "will win." Can you figure out why? The answer is that "will win" is a verb phrase and thus should be put in parentheses.

ESSENTIAL IDEAS IN THIS CHAPTER

- SWAE sentences exhibit flexibility in their structural elements.
- The subordinate clause shows this flexibility in that it can function as three different parts of speech: noun, adjective, and adverb.
- The subordinate clause can also be a subject and an object.
- Sometimes a subordinate clause can disguise itself in what is called the "phrase paradox."
- Clauses can be embedded in phrases and vice versa.

Seven

Verbal Phrases

In chapter 4, phrases were placed into six categories: prepositional, appositive, verb, gerund, participial, and infinitive. The last three phrases are verbal phrases, word groups that derive from verbs but that don't function as verbs in clauses. The distinction between verbs and verbal phrases is crucial for understanding SWAE sentences. Take, for example, a clause with a verb phrase—"Jackson should have gone to his English class." The verb phrase is "should have gone." There are problems, however, if one tries to substitute a verbal phrase for a verb phrase.

For example, one cannot take a gerund phrase—or a present participial phrase, since they resemble one another—and substitute it for the verb phrase: "Jackson going to his English class." Another example is an infinitive phrase: "Jackson to go to his English class." In analyzing these word groups, you need to remember Cardinal Rule #1: *All SWAE sentences must contain at least one main clause.* Furthermore, you need to distinguish between verbs and verbal phrases. The definition of a clause says that it contains a subject-verb relationship, not a subject-*verbal* relationship.

Considering the above, one can make Cardinal Rule #3: *A verbal phrase is not a verb and thus cannot serve as the verb in a clause.* So, for example, the word group "Sophia is learning to play the flute" is a SWAE sentence, while the word group "Sophia learning to play the flute" is not. Verbal phrases do, however, play important roles in SWAE sentences. For example, a gerund phrase functions as a noun and thus can appear in SWAE sentences where one would use a noun.

Here are a few sentences that contain gerund phrases as examples:

1. Finding a good job is becoming more difficult for college graduates.
2. Juanita devoted her energy to finding a good job.
3. Jackie's goal became finding a good job.

In sentence 1, "Finding a good job" is the subject of the verb phrase "is becoming." In sentence 2, "finding a good job" is the object of the preposition "to." In sentence 3, "finding a good job" is a predicate nominative.

Can you find all the clauses and phrases in sentence 1? The most important element of a SWAE sentence is the main clause. In fact, the sentence itself *is* the main clause, so the whole sentence should be bracketed: [Finding a good job is becoming more difficult for college graduates.] Within the main clause—embedded within it—are three phrases: the gerund phrase subject—"Finding a good job"; the verb phrase—"is becoming"; and the prepositional phrase that ends the sentence—"for college graduates." So the sentence can be segmented in this way: [(Finding a good job) (is becoming) more difficult (for college graduates).]

Can you identify the sentence pattern? If you answered that the pattern is subject–linking verb–predicate adjective ("more difficult" is the adjective), you would be correct. To dig a little deeper, the verb phrase is made up of the auxiliary verb "is" and the main verb "becoming," which is a linking verb. The prepositional phrase is composed of the preposition "for" and the object of the preposition—the last word in the phrase—"graduates."

For something a bit trickier, can you find all the embedded phrases in the following sentence: "Working two jobs for the last year of high school, I have had little time for engaging in social activities with my friends."

How many phrases did you find? Did you answer eight?

1. Working two jobs for the last year of high school (participial phrase functioning as adjective modifying the pronoun subject "I")
2. for the last year of high school (prepositional phrase)
3. of high school (prepositional phrase)
4. have had (verb phrase)
5. for engaging in social activities with my friends (prepositional phrase)
6. engaging in social activities with my friends (gerund phrase as object of preposition, "for")
7. in social activities with my friends (prepositional phrase)
8. with my friends (prepositional phrase)

You'll notice that in identifying phrases, one must include the embedded phrase as part of the larger enclosing phrase; thus, "for engaging in social activities with my friends" would first be identified as a prepositional phrase, which also happens to contain other phrases embedded within it. This embedding function is the principal way that SWAE combines both parts of speech and functional grammar in sentence construction.

ESSENTIAL IDEAS IN THIS CHAPTER

- There are three categories of verbal phrases: the gerund, the participial, and the infinitive.
- Verbal phrases are word groups that derive from verbs but that don't function as verbs in clauses.
- Cardinal Rule #3 is that a verbal phrase is not a verb and thus cannot serve as the verb in a clause.
- However, verbal phrases do play important roles in SWAE sentences.
- An example of a verbal phrase playing an important role in SWAE sentences is the gerund phrase.
- A gerund phrase can function as a noun.
- A gerund phrase can thus be a subject, an object, and a predicate nominative.
- Embedding is the principal way that SWAE combines both parts of speech and functional grammar in sentence construction.

Eight

Sentence Patterns

One way to analyze and to write correct SWAE sentences is to categorize them into patterns. Chapter 4 draws a distinction between traditional—or "parts of speech"—grammar and what is called "functional grammar": how clauses and phrases actually work in sentences. This chapter will provide a few different methods for categorizing sentences based on their clause combinations.

In traditional grammar, SWAE sentences are grouped according to the type and number of clauses, both main and subordinate. In this grouping, the type and number of phrases do not affect the grouping. The traditional-grammar sentence patterns are called "simple," "compound," "complex," and "compound-complex."

Simple sentences have one main clause and no subordinate clauses. Thus, the sentence "During class, the students with laptops were doing research on traditional grammar" is simple because it has only one main clause. If you remember the clause patterns in chapter 5, you'll recognize the above main clause as subject–transitive verb–direct object. It's a main clause because it does not have a clause marker and can stand alone. The phrases in the sentence—"During class" (prepositional); "with laptops" (prepositional); "were doing" (verb phrase); "on traditional grammar" (prepositional)—do not affect the grouping, as pointed out above.

Compound sentences have two or more main clauses and no subordinate clauses. One can adapt the above sentence to the form of a compound sentence: "The students were doing research on traditional grammar, and they were using their laptops in class." This is perhaps the most common type of compound sentence, which can be formulated in this way: MC, cc MC. The abbreviation "MC" obviously stands for "main clause," but what does "cc" represent? This abbreviation stands for "coordinating conjunction," a category of words that function as connectors.

One of the traditional parts of speech, conjunctions can connect two clauses of equal grammatical "weight,"—hence, *co*ordinating conjunction—or they can connect clauses of unequal "weight"—a main clause and a subordinate clause, as in the sentence "While the students were in class, they were doing research on traditional grammar on their laptops."

The clause "While the students were in class" is subordinate because of the clause marker "While," which can also be called a subordinating conjunction. This conjunction is one type of clause marker, but there are others as well. For compound sentences, the coordinating conjunctions can be put into an acronym as a memory device: FANBOYS (for, and, nor, but, or, yet, so).

A compound sentence can take on other structural formulas as well. For example, one can rewrite the compound sentence in this way: "The students were doing research on traditional grammar; they were using their laptops in class." The formula for this sentence is MC; MC. Another formula has this pattern: MC; tw MC (or MC; tw, MC, with the comma being optional); "tw" is an abbreviation for "transitional word" or "transitional words." The tw category embraces many words and phrases that are common in SWAE sentences: "however," "nevertheless," "consequently," "moreover," "therefore," "then," "thus" (these are also called "conjunctive adverbs"); and "for example," "for instance," "on the other hand" (which are also prepositional phrases used to connect clauses).

Most compound sentences can be rewritten as simple sentences; for example, the compound sentence "The students were doing research on traditional grammar; they were using their laptops in class" can be rewritten this way: "The students were doing research on traditional grammar. They were using their laptops in class." In the same way, one can rewrite the first sentence in this paragraph by putting a period at the end of the first clause, after "simple sentences," and then capitalizing "for example."

An analysis of the compound sentence pattern—MC, cc MC—can help clear up a very common misconception about the coordinating conjunctions "and" and "but." In the paragraph that introduced compound sentences, this sentence is used as an example: "The students were doing research on traditional grammar, and they were using their laptops in class." If one were to rewrite this sentence as two simple sentences, they would look like this: "The students were doing research on traditional grammar. And they were using their laptops in class."

When students are shown this rewrite, many of them object to the transformation, claiming, "You can't start a sentence with 'and' or 'but.'" They have usually heard this bit of "urban legend" grammar from their high school English teachers. Now, one does not want to indict all high school English teachers for misinforming their students, but this objection is heard so much that one could conclude there is a conspiracy going on!

This misconception can be cleared up once and for all—a nice cliché for this falsehood! You can start a sentence with any word you want—as long as it is a SWAE sentence. You can also start a sentence with the subordinating conjunction "because," which is another "forbidden" word, according to some students. This sentence should be written on the blackboard—or whiteboard—by all English teachers: "Because I am tired of hearing this nonsense about 'because,' I am requiring you to write at least five sentences in your next paper, all of them beginning with that word."

ESSENTIAL IDEAS IN THIS CHAPTER

- In traditional grammar, SWAE sentences are classified according to the type and number of main and subordinate clauses.
- Phrases are not used to classify sentences.
- A simple sentence has one main clause and no subordinate clauses.
- A compound sentence has two or more main clauses and no subordinate clauses.
- A complex sentence has one main and one or more subordinate clauses.
- A compound-complex sentence has two or more main and one or more subordinate clauses.
- The compound sentence can have a variety of structural formulas.
- Contrary to popular opinion, SWAE sentences can begin with "and," "but," and "because."

NINE

Additional Clause Patterns

In the previous chapter, compound sentences were examined, as well as a subordinate-clause sentence pattern, beginning with the clause marker "because" (which can also be called a "subordinating conjunction"). It would be helpful at this point to examine some sentence patterns that use subordinate and main clauses. Sentences that have one main clause and one or more subordinate clauses are called "complex" in traditional grammar classification.

Here's a complex sentence that begins with the clause marker "when": "When I get up in the morning, I have a specific routine based on my first cup of coffee." The complex sentence formula of SC, MC can be used to describe this type of sentence. Of course, you can usually reverse the order of the clauses to make the pattern MC SC: "I have a specific routine based on my first cup of coffee when I get up in the morning." When you use this pattern, you can omit the comma after the main clause.

Some complex sentences, however, have a fixed clause order that precludes switching the clauses around. The pattern—M SC C—illustrated by the sentence "The injury that I sustained in basketball has prevented me from playing other sports," has a fixed clause structure. Thus you would not be able to write the sentence in this way: "The injury has prevented me from playing other sports that I sustained in basketball." The formula M SC C may look confusing at first, but once you understand that the subordinate clause is sandwiched within the main clause, you'll have an easier time understanding the pattern.

Another common complex sentence pattern follows the formula SC, MC SC: "When I woke up this morning, my back hurt even though I stretched the night before." Some writers would prefer a comma after "hurt," making the formula look like this: SC, MC, SC. When it comes to commas, there are many conflicting opinions and usages. The old adage about commas, "When in doubt, leave them out," is not bad advice, but there are places where a comma is required in SWAE usage.

For example, when the subordinate clause begins a sentence, a comma is required—as evidenced by the sentence that is being composed at this minute! One amazing thing about SWAE sentences is their flexibility: you can twist, turn, and transform the phrase and clause patterns and formulas to suit your needs.

For example, the above sentence—"When I woke up this morning, my back hurt even though I stretched the night before"—can be transformed in this way: make the opening subordinate clause a present participial phrase. If you need to review verbal phrases, go back to chapter 7 for a quick review. If you don't need to review, then here's the transformation: the clause "When I woke up this morning" gets transformed into "Waking up this morning." The main clause, though—"my back hurt"—can't stand unchanged since the sentence would contain what's called a "dangling modifier," or, to be more precise, "a dangling participle."

How many jokes and wisecracks have evolved from this most common SWAE error! A very clever stand-up comic once used this error in his closing remarks—to a convention of English teachers: "And remember this sage advice: don't ever let your participle dangle!"

Completing the transformation—and avoiding making the participial phrase modify "my back"—the main clause is changed to "I felt pain in my back." The sentence now reads, "Waking up this morning, I felt pain in my back." We can add the subordinate clause—"even though I stretched the night before"—to the end of the sentence.

Learning the structural formulas of traditional grammar classification does not mean that writers think of the formulas as they are writing. In other words, writers don't say to themselves as they are composing, "I think I'll construct my next paragraph of four simple, three complex, and one compound-complex sentence." Rather, writers have the sentence patterns internalized, as part of their toolbox or sentence repertoire.

When they compose sentences, most writers try to use a variety of patterns to give some style to their sentences and paragraphs. Because they know the "rules" of SWAE sentence construction, they can choose to combine clauses and phrases to create a SWAE sentences that is different from the ones they just wrote. The two previous sentences can stand as an examples. Both sentences start off with subordinate clauses "when they compose" and "because they know."

It would be monotonous to write a third sentence with this opening SC construction, so a compound sentence with the pattern MC, cc MC is a good choice. If you look at the previous sentence, it has that pattern. Understanding the elements of both traditional and functional grammar will help you become proficient in SWAE.

Additional Clause Patterns

Will you be a great writer—or even a good writer—if you learn this material? Maybe—or maybe not. But you can be a "correct" writer, someone who knows the rules and who knows how to utilize them.

The compound-complex pattern is made up of two or more main clauses and one or more subordinate clauses. This structure can be likened to juggling three balls, while the simple, the complex, and the compound can be compared to juggling one or two.

Here's one formula for juggling three balls: SC, MC, cc MC. This is a very familiar pattern for anyone who writes regularly. If you write every day, you probably have used this pattern, and you can vary it. That last sentence is an example of the compound-complex pattern: the SC is "If you write every day"; the two main clauses are "you probably have used this pattern" and "you can vary it." The cc is "and."

Here's a variation: "If you write every day, you probably have used this pattern; you can vary it as well." This is the formula: SC, MC; MC. As a variation, "as well" is used to express the idea of "and" from the first sentence. Of course, you can separate the clauses and make a complex and a simple sentence. Why don't you take a minute to adapt the SC, MC, cc MC to a complex and simple sentence looking like this: SC, MC. MC.

If you tried and are now back, here is one version: "If you write every day, you probably have used this pattern. And you can vary it." Don't forget that "and" is a coordinating conjunction and thus can legitimately start a main clause, unlike "if," which is a subordinating conjunction and thus turns the clause into a subordinate clause. Here are a few patterns for compound-complex sentences:

MC, cc MC SC.
SC, MC, cc, MC.
SC, MC; MC.
SC, MC; tw, MC.
SC, MC SC.

ESSENTIAL IDEAS IN THIS CHAPTER

- Complex and compound-complex sentences can have a variety of structures.
- Comma usage in compound and compound-complex sentences can be confusing.
- Accomplished writers of SWAE don't necessarily think of sentence patterns when they are writing.

Ten

The Flexible Phrase

If you can recall chapter 8, you may remember that sentence patterns are based on the number of clauses. However, phrases do play an important part in SWAE sentence construction. In chapter 9, the subordinate clause "When I wake up in the morning" was transformed into the present participial phrase "Waking up in the morning" in order to provide variety to sentence patterns. This kind of transformation makes sentence construction in SWAE extremely flexible—if you follow the "rules."

The following are some phrase transformations: "My high school English teacher, who was chairman of the department, always wore suits to class." Can you identify the sentence pattern? If you said that the pattern is a complex sentence in the form M SC C, you would be correct. Can you convert the subordinate clause into an appositive phrase? Would your sentence look like this: "My high school English teacher, the chairman of the department, always wore suits to class"?

Let's try another sentence: "The house that was on the corner burned down last night." Again, this is the complex sentence pattern: M SC C. Can you convert the subordinate clause to a prepositional phrase? Your sentence should look like this: "The house on the corner burned down last night."

If you recall from chapter 4, phrases were placed into six categories: prepositional, appositive, verb, gerund, participial (both past and present), and infinitive. It is important to note that a verbal phrase cannot function as a verb in a clause. But a *verb phrase* can. The following are examples of sentences with verbal phrases as the verbs in the clause: "Beverly to diet strictly all week," or "Beverly dieting faithfully all week." These clearly are not SWAE sentences. Why? They don't have a subject-verb relationship.

One can convert the preceding sentences into SWAE sentences by adding verb phrases: "Beverly should have dieted strictly all week," and "Beverly was dieting faithfully all week." Now that you have clarified the difference between a verb phrase and a verbal phrase, try to convert the subordinate clause in the following sentence to an infinitive phrase: "If you are interested in making a lot of money, you should consider investing in the stock market."

The subordinate clause is "If you are interested in making a lot of money," and the clause can be converted to this infinitive phrase: "To make a lot of money." So now the sentence reads, "To make a lot of money, you should consider investing in the stock market."

Notice that the introductory infinitive phrase, when it's used as a modifier (of "you"), is followed by a comma. However, when the phrase is used as a noun and is acting like a subject of the verb, the phrase is not followed by a comma: "To make a lot of money comes easier for some than for others."

Learning to use phrases correctly will give you flexibility in SWAE sentence construction. Phrases, for example, can combine traditional parts-of-speech grammar with functional grammar, in sentences like the following:

1. *Learning the elements of SWAE* is important if you are a student. (Gerund phrase used as a noun and the subject of the verb "is.")
2. I wanted *to learn the elements of SWAE*. (Infinitive phrase used as a noun and the direct object of the verb "wanted.")
3. The house *on the corner* burned down last night. (Prepositional phrase used as adjective modifying the noun "house.")
4. *Taking his last final*, Bernard felt a lot of pressure. (Present participial phrase used as adjective modifying the noun "Bernard.")
5. I gave *running a marathon* one more chance. (Gerund phrase used as a noun and the indirect object of the verb "gave.")

Prepositional phrases are ubiquitous in SWAE sentences. This is a propitious time for a digression to point out the vocabulary of SWAE sentences, which is characterized by words that you would probably not use in your everyday, "colloquial" dialect. Both "ubiquitous" and "propitious" are examples of such vocabulary. Using a more educated vocabulary does not mean that you have to consult a thesaurus for every word you use, but it does mean that you should make an effort to enrich your vocabulary.

Back to prepositional phrases, which are ubiquitous (defined as "existing or being everywhere," per Dictionary.com) in SWAE sentences. As seen above, prepositional phrases can function as adjectives—"The car in the driveway is brand new"; and as adverbs—"To run in a marathon is now my goal." Prepositional phrases are frequently embedded in other phrases, as is the case in the previous sentence. Can you recognize the embedded phrases in the previous sentence? If you answered, "To run in a marathon," you would be correct: the prepositional phrase "in a marathon" is embedded in the infinitive phrase "To run in a marathon."

Take a moment to examine the sentence above: "To run in a marathon is now my goal." How much can you explain about this sentence using the information from the previous chapters of this book? Start with the basics. Is this a SWAE sentence? Yes, it is. Why? It has a main clause. Try to take the main clause apart. Find the verb first. Did you identify the verb as "is"? What kind of verb is this? It's a "'to be' verb." What is the subject of the verb? Did you say, "To run in a marathon"? That's correct. The subject is an infinitive phrase with an embedded prepositional phrase.

To classify the clause, one would say it is classification #6 (from chapter 5): subject–"to be" verb–predicate nominative. The predicate nominative is the noun "goal." Are you following so far? If so, try to identify the sentence pattern. Remember that sentence patterns are categorized based on the type and number of clauses. So how many clauses and what type are they in "To run in a marathon is now my goal"? There is one main clause and no subordinate clause. So this information helps to classify the sentence as a simple sentence.

The only word in the sentence that has not been identified is "now," which is an adverb, using the "parts-of-speech" category. Adverbs can be single words, phrases, and even clauses; and they answer the questions "When?," "In what manner?," "Where?," and "To what extent?"

Now that you have examined the structure and function of clauses and phrases in SWAE sentences, it is time to shift gears a bit and look at sentences that violate the "rules" of Standard Written American English. Knowing what is right about SWAE sentences will now help you to understand what goes wrong with SWAE sentences.

ESSENTIAL IDEAS IN THIS CHAPTER

- Phrases play an important role in SWAE sentences.
- Phrases provide variety to sentence patterns.
- There is a difference between a verbal phrase and a verb phrase.
- A verb phrase can function as the verb in a clause, but a verbal phrase cannot.
- Phrases can combine traditional parts-of-speech grammar with functional grammar.

PART II

Eleven

The Big Three

The end of chapter 2 stated that learning about SWAE is more than understanding what is wrong with sentences; it is also realizing what is right about sentences. Consequently, part I examined sentences that mostly adhered to the rules of SWAE sentence construction. In part II, however, sentences that break the rules in various ways will be analyzed. Remember the two major characteristics of SWAE: it's rule-bound, and it's conservative.

In a sense, learning to navigate the rules of SWAE is like learning to drive a car and observing the rules of the road, which don't change very often. If you go over the speed limit or if you run a red light, you risk getting a ticket and paying a fine. Now it must be said that since English—like other living languages—is constantly changing, its "rules" are changing too. However, the rules of SWAE change more slowly than those of the other dialects of English. It is hoped that what you learned about phrases and clauses in part I will help you understand why errors occur and how to fix them.

With that in mind, one should start with what are often called the "Big Three" sentence structure errors: comma splices, fused sentences, and fragments. You may be accustomed to different terminology for these errors. The first two—comma splices and fused sentences—are sometimes called "run-ons," while the fragment is often referred to as an "incomplete sentence." Whatever they are called, these errors are called the "Big Three" because they are considered the most serious writing errors, ones that reveal the writer's weak grasp of the principles of SWAE sentence structure.

In fact, some people—mostly English teachers!—consider these such serious errors that they are called "fatal errors." Some English teachers would give an F to a paper that contained just one of the fatal errors, no matter how good the rest of the paper was. However, it is an axiom of SWAE that no one element of writing should outweigh all the others.

In relation to the sentence fragment, which was discussed in chapters 3 and 4, this error violates Cardinal Rules #1 and #2: All SWAE sentences must contain at least one main clause; and phrases, by themselves, no matter how long, cannot be considered SWAE sentences. It has been pointed out, however, that many writers use fragments in their works.

At this point, it may be helpful to distinguish between different genres, or types, of writing. A very general distinction can be made between fiction and nonfiction. Fiction, sometimes called imaginative literature, includes novels, short stories, poetry, and drama, while nonfiction can refer to essays, historical works, memoirs, biographies, autobiographies, journalism, and criticism.

Generally speaking, the rules of SWAE can be bent or even violated in fictional works, especially in poetry; on the other hand, nonfiction usually adheres more strictly to the rules of SWAE. Why this seemingly contradictory practice takes place can't be addressed here since it's too complicated to analyze. Here is an excerpt of a poem by Don Marquis that violates many of the rules of SWAE:

mehitabel s morals

boss I got
a message from
mehitabel the cat
the other day
brought me by
a cockroach
she asks for our help
it seems she is being
held at ellis
island while an
investigation is made
of her morals[1]

Certainly the success of this witty poem can't be judged by the rules of SWAE. In fact, the very success of the poem is that it flagrantly breaks the rules!

Of the "Big Three" errors discussed above, the one that is most common is the fragment, perhaps because it can resemble a SWAE sentence. Here is an example from the magnificent biography *Alexander Hamilton*, by Ron Chernow: "A glowing tribute from a man who had observed Hamilton at close range for four years."[2] At first glance, this seems like a SWAE sentence: it has a subject and verb—"who" and "had observed." But it doesn't have the main requisite for a SWAE sentence: a main clause.

The word "who," if you remember from chapter 3, is a clause marker that introduces a subordinate cause. Chernow probably made the decision that a fragment offered variety to his sentences, especially since the meaning is quite clear. Since the fragment follows a quotation that praises

Hamilton, Chernow could have written, "This is a glowing tribute from a man who had observed Hamilton at close range for four years." But he clearly believed that a fragment stated the idea more succinctly.

The point here is that using a fragment is acceptable *if*—and this is a big if—you know that you are using it. It's probably wiser to obey the rules if you are a novice writer who is just learning the rules of SWAE.

One type of fragment that seems to be garnering acceptance in the writing community is the subordinate clause construction beginning with the clause marker "which." Here is an example from an online tutorial of the "which" fragment: "The current city policy on housing is incomplete as it stands. Which is why we believe the proposed amendment should be passed." The analysis of this usage points out that it is practiced mainly by newspaper and magazine journalists but is mostly avoided by academic writers and by those who are involved in more formal writing.[3]

Most academic writers, who adhere strictly to the rules of SWAE, usually avoid this type of construction. Which is true for most colleagues in the college writing community. Did you notice something about the last sentence? If you answered that it is a fragment, then you are grasping SWAE principles! Lately, however, the "which" fragment is creeping into academic writing, so the construction may be one of those that demonstrates that language changes, even SWAE. Here are a few examples:

> Esther Shore, *Bridge of Words: Esperanto and the Dream of a Universal Language* (2016): "God's crowning revenge on the builders of Babel was the choice of Israel, and there, on Israel, God's attention rested, leaving the rabbis of the Talmud to finish off the builders of Babel. Which they most certainly did, declaring 'the generation of the scattered' personae non gratae in the world to come."[4]

> Warren Berger, *A More Beautiful Question: The Power of Inquiry to Spark Breakthrough Ideas* (2014): "But eventually, all doctors—and all the rest of us, as well—will have access to some form of cloud-based super-search-engine that can quickly answer almost any factual question with a level of precision and expertise that's way beyond what we have now. Which reinforces that the value of questions is going to keep rising as that of answers keeps falling."[5]

Of course, both Shore and Berger could have chosen another way of expressing their ideas without resorting to fragments. The point is, though, that both authors *knew* they were "violating" the rules, but they chose the "which" clause as a stylistic device to give some variety to their sentences. But if you're a novice SWAE student, it's best to play the game according to the rules.

When it comes to the other "Big Three" errors, the comma splice and fused sentence, one is not dealing with word groups that lack a main clause. To the contrary, these two errors involve sentences that have two or more main clauses and sometimes one or more subordinate clauses.

Chapter 8 looked at classification of sentences based on the number and type of clauses. If you recall the classifications, you will remember that a simple sentence has one main clause and no subordinate clauses; a complex sentence has one main clause and one or more subordinate clauses; a compound sentence has two or more main clauses and no subordinate clauses; and a compound-complex sentence has two or more main clauses and one or more subordinate clauses.

So if you apply the description of the comma splice and fused sentence errors to the sentence classifications, you'll realize that the errors can occur only in a compound and/or a compound-complex sentence. The following are a few examples, starting with the comma splice:

> I wanted to see the new movie at the Cedar-Lee Theater, however the showtimes weren't convenient for me.
> There was a serious problem with the new projection system, the bulbs burned out too quickly.

Both of these examples are actually compound sentences that are incorrectly punctuated. The first one most likely occurs because of confusion between a coordinating conjunction and a conjunctive adverb. If you remember, a conjunctive adverb is a type of transitional word that occurs in compound sentences that can have the pattern MC; tw, MC, which is often confused with the pattern MC, cc MC, with the cc representing a coordinating conjunction.

The coordinating conjunctions are the only ones that can take a comma before them; the transitional words require a semicolon—or a period, if you are writing two simple sentences. So here is the correct sentence with the pattern MC; tw, MC: "I wanted to see the new movie at the Cedar-Lee Theater; however, the showtimes weren't convenient for me." And here is the correct sentence with the pattern MC, cc MC: "I wanted to see the new movie at the Cedar-Lee Theater, but the showtimes weren't convenient for me." Of course, you could also write the sentence these ways:

> "I wanted to see the new movie at the Cedar-Lee Theater. However, the showtimes weren't convenient for me."
> "I wanted to see the new film at the Cedar-Lee Theater. But the showtimes weren't convenient for me."

In relation to commas, one should remember this bit of sage advice: "When in doubt, leave them out." However, there are a few places you shouldn't be in doubt; one of them is this pattern: MC, cc MC. In the pattern MC; tw, MC, however, some writers would omit the comma after "however," and some writers would omit it in writing the above sentence this way: "I wanted to see the new film at the Cedar-Lee Theater but the showtimes weren't convenient for me." This sentence, to some writers' way of thinking, is not correctly punctuated, but the usage is one of those gray areas that seem to characterize punctuation in general.

The second comma splice error—represented by the formula MC, MC—offers another conundrum (good SWAE word!) for writers of SWAE. It seems that the choice of punctuation can depend on the length of the clauses. For example, the translation of Julius Caesar's famous line in Latin, "Veni, vidi, vici," is "I came, I saw, I conquered." According to our criteria above, these would be considered comma splices, but because the clauses are brief and balanced—they have the same number of words in the same order—they are frequently separated by commas.

In these cases, novice SWAE students should stick to the "rules" and use these patterns:

MC. MC
MC, cc MC
MC; MC
MC; tw, MC.

In the example from Julius Caesar, you could write, "I came. I saw. I conquered." Or you could write, "I came; I saw; I conquered." To reiterate, SWAE always presents you with solutions to problems in sentence construction—that is, if you know the rules of the game.

The last of the "Big Three" sentence errors is the fused sentence, probably the least common of the three. Here are two examples drawn from the sample sentences above:

> I wanted to see the new movie at the Cedar-Lee Theater however the showtimes weren't convenient for me.
> There was a serious problem with the new projection system the bulbs burned out too quickly.

Again, the problem occurs only with compound or compound-complex sentences. Can you categorize the two sentences above? If you said they are compound sentences, you would be correct. The correction for the above errors is similar to that for the comma splice error. For the first sentence, you can use the pattern MC; tw, MC: "I wanted to see the new movie at the Cedar-Lee Theater; however, the showtimes weren't convenient for me." And for the second sentence, you can use MC; MC: "There was a serious problem with the new projection system; the bulbs burned out too quickly."

Of course, since the sentence is a compound one, you can always make the main clauses into their own sentences:

> I wanted to see the new movie at the Cedar-Lee Theater. However, the showtimes weren't convenient for me.
> There was a serious problem with the new projection system. The bulbs burned out too quickly.

And then there is the old standby, MC, cc MC: "I wanted to see the new film at the Cedar-Lee Theater, but the showtimes weren't convenient for me."

Some overly fussy English teachers might insist that without a comma before "but," the above sentence would be a fused sentence. In other words, the pattern MC cc MC is fused. This, however, is not the case since the coordinating conjunction "but" keeps the clauses from being fused. In fact, some writers leave out the comma in this kind of pattern just to avoid using too many commas in their writing. But to be on the safe side, always use a comma in the MC, cc MC compound sentence pattern.

One other solution to the fused sentence and comma splice error is to consider subordination, which means converting one of the main clauses to a subordinate clause. In effect, you would be converting a compound sentence into a complex one (or a compound-complex one) and thus solving the problem. Try to apply subordination to one of the sentence examples above:

> Because the showtimes weren't convenient for me, I wasn't able to see the new film at the Cedar-Lee Theater.

Or:

> I wasn't able to see the new film at the Cedar-Lee Theater because the show times weren't convenient for me.

You'll notice that the wording was altered a bit in order to accommodate the new pattern. The meaning, however, stays the same. You might also notice that the punctuation changed from one sentence to the other. The first has the pattern SC, MC, while the second is MC SC. Both patterns are examples of the complex sentence. The SC, MC requires a comma after the introductory subordinate clause, while the MC SC does not.

But—isn't there always a "but" in SWAE?—if the subordinate clause begins with a clause marker like "although" or "even though," some writers would put a comma before the subordinate clause. Here's an example: "The projector bulbs burned out quickly, even though the system was brand-new."

To review the chapter on the "Big Three" sentence errors, you can apply your solutions to a sentence that contains a comma splice or fused sentence error and then to a sentence that contains a fragment error.

> Alfred Hitchcock made many films over his fifty-year career, he never won an Academy Award for Best Director.

Apply the following formulas for correcting the error above:

MC, cc MC.
MC; MC.
MC; tw, MC. (or MC, tw MC.)
MC. MC.
SC, MC.

Can you identify the error? If you said comma splice, you would be correct.

MC, cc MC.

- Alfred Hitchcock made many films over his fifty-year career, but he never won an Academy Award for Best Director.

MC; MC.

- Alfred Hitchcock made many films over his fifty-year career; he never won an Academy Award for Best Director.

MC; tw, MC. (or MC; tw MC)

- Alfred Hitchcock made many films over his fifty-year career; however, he never won an Academy Award for Best Director.

MC. MC.

- Alfred Hitchcock made many films over his fifty-year career. He never won an Academy Award for Best Director.

SC, MC.

- Although Alfred Hitchcock made many films over his fifty-year career, he never won an Academy Award for Best Director.

Of course, there are other formulas for correcting the comma splice. For example, you could use this one: MC. Tw, MC.

Alfred Hitchcock made many films over his fifty-year career. However, he never won an Academy Award for Best Director.

Or you could choose this one: MC. Cc MC.

Alfred Hitchcock made many films over his fifty-year career. But he never won an Academy Award for Best Director.

When it comes to the fragment error, you have several options, depending on the type of fragment. Here's an example: "Alfred Hitchcock never won an Academy Award for Best director. Even though he made over fifty films in his long career." Can you find the fragment? If you remember Cardinal Rule #1, you should have no trouble identifying the word group beginning with "Even though" as the fragment. In order to be a SWAE sentence, a word group must contain at least one main clause. The word group "Even though he made over fifty films in his long career" is a fragment because it lacks a main clause.

Let's try a few ways to correct the error. One way—perhaps the simplest—is to connect the subordinate clause to the nearest main clause that it has a connection to. Here's the correction: "Alfred Hitchcock never won an Academy Award for Best Director, even though he made over fifty films in his long career." Another possibility is to add to—or subtract from—the subordinate clause: "Alfred Hitchcock never won an Academy Award for Best Director. He made over fifty films in his long career." In some senses, this is a less satisfactory solution to the fragment error because the logical connection represented by "even though" is missing. However, the fragment error is corrected.

Another kind of fragment occurs as a result of the violation of Cardinal Rule #2: A phrase, no matter how long, cannot be a SWAE sentence. Here's an example: "At the end of a long career of making one great film after another. Alfred Hitchcock was finally given a Lifetime Achievement Award by the Academy."

Did you identify the first word group as a fragment? If you did, good for you! The first word group is a series of phrases lacking a main clause. Here are the phrases:

"At the end": prepositional phrase
"of a long career": prepositional phrase
"of making one great film": prepositional phrase
"making one great film": gerund phrase
"after another": prepositional phrase

As long as you saw that there was not a main clause in the word group, don't worry if you were not able to name the phrases. The correction is simple in this case: place a comma after "another." Now you have a word group that passes muster as a SWAE sentence: "At the end of a long career of making one great film after another, Alfred Hitchcock was finally given a Lifetime Achievement Award by the Academy."

By the way, can you categorize the above sentence? If you said simple, you would be correct. Many times a very long sentence like the above can be "simply a simple" sentence because it contains only one main clause.

ESSENTIAL IDEAS IN THIS CHAPTER

- The "Big Three" writing errors are considered the most serious.
- The "Big Three" errors are the fragment, the comma splice, and the fused sentence.
- A fragment is a word group that lacks a main clause.
- Many accomplished writers use fragments in their writing.
- A distinction can be made between fiction and nonfiction writing.
- Errors in SWAE are frequently made in fiction writing: novels, short stories, poetry, and drama.
- Nonfiction—essays, historical works, memoirs, biographies, journalism, and criticism—usually adheres more strictly to the rules of SWAE.
- In nonfiction, writers sometimes employ fragments for stylistic effects.
- Comma splices and fused sentences, unlike fragments, have main clauses, but they are not punctuated correctly.
- The fused sentence is the least common of the "Big Three" sentence errors.
- There are several formulas for correcting the comma splice and fused sentence errors.
- The way to correct the fragment error is to add a main clause to the word group.

NOTES

1. Don Marquis, "mehitabel s morals," https://tuitalk.wordpress.com/2011/05/10/tuesday-poem-mehitabel-s-morals-by-don-marquis/ (accessed December 5, 2017).

2. Ron Chernow, *Alexander Hamilton* (New York: Penguin Books, 2004), 155.

3. Rebecca Oberg, "Using Sentence Fragments Wisely," http://www.sophia.org/tutorials/using-sentence-fragments-wisely (accessed December 10, 2017).

4. Esther Shore, *Bridge of Words: Esperanto and the Dream of a Universal Language* (New York: Metropolitan Books, 2016), 19.

5. Warren Berger, *A More Beautiful Question: The Power of Inquiry to Spark Breakthrough Ideas* (New York: Bloomsbury USA, 2014), 27.

Twelve

Agreement I
Subjects and Verbs

No other characteristic of sentences seems to cause more problems than the subject-verb relationship. It's probably the first concept that is taught in English classes—or in language arts classes, as they are called in many schools. A traditional way to analyze sentences is the Reed-Kellogg sentence diagramming exercise, during which students have to analyze sentences by drawing lines bisecting and connecting sentence elements.

The first line underscores the whole sentence, and then the next line is a vertical one dividing the subject from the predicate (Latinate term for "verb"). Hence, the sentence "Juanita likes her new English teacher" would look like this:

Juanita | likes her new English teacher.

Other lines would be drawn to identify direct objects, predicate nominatives, and so forth. Some of the lines would be diagonal ones drawn below the main line and intersecting it. For a complicated sentence with many clauses and phrases, the diagram would end up looking like an insane family tree!

Many teachers believe, however, that Reed-Kellogg diagramming makes sentence analysis much too complicated and that it does little to advance understanding of SWAE and the various errors that occur when trying to observe the rules. If one approaches sentence structure from the clause/phrase angle, however, one can learn quite a bit about how that structure works and how it doesn't work.

The previous chapters talked a great deal about the structure and function of clauses. One of the important concepts is this definition: "A clause is a group of related words with a subject-verb relationship." You are now going to examine this relationship in some detail as an introduction to errors that occur within this relationship. The major characteristic of the subject-verb relationship is called "agreement," which means that the verb must agree with the subject in number: if the subject is singular, the verb must be singular as well.

For a sentence like "Juanita likes her new English teacher," the agreement seems easy: "Juanita" is singular, and the verb matches it in number, "likes." As in most clauses, if one element is changed, others change as well. So if "Juanita" is changed to "The students"—in other words, if the subject is made plural—the verb must also change to plural: "The students like their new English teacher." You'll notice that another change had to be made as well. The plural "students" requires a plural pronoun that refers back to the noun, so "her" must be changed to "their."

If one makes another modification to the sentence by changing "Juanita" to "Juan," the pronoun must change to reflect the change in gender of the noun: "Juan likes his new English teacher." Pronouns will be examined in the next chapter, where it will be revealed that "agreement" refers not only to subjects and verbs but also to pronouns and their antecedents (a fancy word for the word the pronoun refers to and takes the place of).

The concept of agreement is something most people take for granted in their use of language, but it is a fascinating and complex process that occurs in most languages. In chapter 4, English was classified as an analytical language as opposed to an inflectional language like Latin. However, as important as word order is in English, there are inflectional characteristics in our language. Agreement is one example of inflection.

If you change "The students" to the singular "The student," you've begun a complicated inflectional process that requires you to drop the "s" from "The students" and then add the "s" to the verb "like." Hence, the sentence now reads, "The student likes his or her new teacher."

You'll notice an additional change: the singular pronoun "his" or "her," although appropriate when the gender of the noun is known (Juan or Juanita), changes to "his or her" to reflect the nongendered "The student." The change made in the pronoun reflects not a grammatical alteration, since the pronoun is still singular, but rather a social change dictated by avoiding gender bias in language.

In the above sentences, the "s" represents an inflectional component of subjects and verbs. In the children's book titled *That Pesky S*, a young boy named Jed tries to outwit his eccentric English-teacher dad. Jed's father, Mr. Simon, has been running around the house yelling, "That Pesky S," and Jed sets out to find out what that statement means.[1]

The story has a serious side to it. In trying to uncover the meaning of "That Pesky S," Jed learns a lot about the role of the letter "s" in the inflectional structure of English. So if you put the subject-verb relationship into the context of inflection, you will realize that if an error occurs in that relationship, it is due to a kind of "short circuit" in that relationship. Look at this example:

The cost of all the groceries are much more than I can afford.

At first glance, we may think there is nothing wrong with the sentence. The verb "are" follows the plural noun "groceries." However, the noun "groceries" is not the subject of the verb "are." In effect, there's a mistake going on in the inflection of the verb. Because we usually find the subject of the verb placed before the verb, it is easy to make a mistake.

If you go back a few chapters to the analysis of clauses and phrases, you may remember that phrases can be embedded in clauses and vice versa. If you analyze the clause/phrase structure of the sentence, you might be able to see how the error occurs.

The sentence has two clauses: the main clause is "The cost of all the groceries are much more," and the subordinate clause is "than I can afford." The sentence, then, can be classified as a complex sentence; consequently, since there are two clauses in this particular sentence, there are two subject-verb relationships. The one in the subordinate clause is correct: the pronoun subject "I" agrees with the verb phrase "can afford." The main clause, as noted above, contains the subject-verb agreement error.

The main clause should look like this: "The cost of all the groceries is much more." Let's see if you can figure out how this agreement error takes place. The key to the agreement error lies in the concepts of embedding and inflection. If the "rule" about the necessity of making verbs agree with subjects in number is combined with the function of embedding, you can find the answer and fix the error.

The verb of the main clause, as noted above, is a singular noun, "cost." If you recall the discussion of subjects and verbs in chapters 3 and 4, you will remember that you get the subject by finding the verb and then asking, "Who or what ____?" So in the clause with the error, you ask of the verb, "What is much more?" The answer is "cost," which is a singular noun, not "groceries," which is a plural noun.

Can you figure out how the noun "groceries" works in the sentence? It's the object in the prepositional phrase "of all the groceries," which is embedded in the main clause. And if a word or word group is functioning as an object, it can't also be a subject.

It's easy to make this error partly because English is mainly an analytical language and is dependent on word order. So you usually find the subject before the verb, as in the sentence "The student wrote a research paper," with "student" being the subject of the verb "wrote." But in the clause with the error, it's easy to write "groceries cost," because "groceries" is positioned before the verb and thus seems like the subject.

Now that you hopefully understand the subject-verb agreement error, you can look at a few iterations (a good SWAE word) of that error.

Each of the students were on the bus.

This error is a combination of two concepts: embedding (prepositional phrase embedded in the main clause) and pronoun usage. The first concept was already discussed above, but the second, pronoun usage, needs some explanation. Pronouns are extremely inflectional: they change their form based on their function. In addition, pronouns are placed in several categories, some of which may sound familiar.

One such category is called "indefinite pronouns": each, everybody, nobody, everyone, someone, one, everything, something, many, most, none, all. This is not an exhaustive list, but those listed cause most of the problems. The pronoun "each" is one of them. Many of the indefinite pronouns, "each" included, take singular verbs. For example, in the sentence above, since "each" is singular, the verb must be singular as well. So the sentence should read, "Each of the students was on the bus." To many students, this correction doesn't sound right, mainly because the word "students" is plural, and it sounds incorrect to write "students was."

However, if you remember the earlier analysis of subject-verb agreement, something that is an object—in this case "students"—can't be a subject as well. Many of the indefinite pronouns take singular verbs: each, everybody, nobody, somebody, someone, one. To make things a bit more complicated, a few of the indefinite pronouns can take singular or plural verbs, depending on the context. For example, the pronoun "all," which seems plural, can take a singular noun if "all" refers to an amount, not a number. The following are a few sentences that use "all" correctly:

All of the actors were at the audition.
All of the money was recovered.

In each sentence, the pronoun stays the same, but the verb is plural in the first sentence and singular in the second. It may seem paradoxical to use the object of the preposition to make a determination of the number of the subject since you shouldn't confuse objects with subjects. However, in the two cases above, you need to consider the object of the preposition in order to make the right determination about the number of the subject. There are a few other indefinite pronouns that are like "all": "most" and "none" are the most common.

A third subject-verb agreement error involves a special kind of conjunction called a "correlative conjunction." In chapter 9, we discussed subordinating conjunctions, which are clause markers introducing subordinate clauses. Common subordinating conjunctions are "because," "although," "even though," and "if," among others. Then there are coordinating conjunctions, which link main clauses and which are abbreviated with the acronym FANBOYS.

Correlative conjunctions are the third type of conjunction, and they come in pairs, "neither . . . nor," and "either . . . or." Because there are two of them, they frequently cause problems in subject-verb agreement. Let's see if you can figure out what the number of the verb should be in the following sentences:

> Neither the professor nor the student know/knows the solution to the problem.
> Neither the professor nor the students know/knows the solution to the problem.
> Either the lawyers or the prosecutors is/are responsible for the mistrial.
> Either the prosecutors or the lawyer is/are responsible for the mistrial.

As you are trying to figure out what the correct answers are, here are a few guidelines that might help. Just remember that SWAE is both conservative and rule-bound, so the guidelines may seem arbitrary and perhaps contradictory, but these guidelines are just "rules of the game"!

- The correlative conjunctions do *not* make the subject plural, even though there seem to be two subjects. The verb will remain singular *if* both subjects are singular.
- If both subjects are plural themselves, then the verb will be plural.
- If one of the subjects is singular and one is plural, the verb will agree with the subject nearer in word order to the verb.

Now that you have the guidelines, you can tackle each sentence in order.

> Neither the professor nor the student knows the solution to the problem.

Since each subject is a singular noun, the verb remains singular.

> Neither the professor nor the students know the solution to the problem.

Since one subject is singular and one is plural, the verb agrees with the one closer in word order to the verb. In this sentence, "students" is closer to the verb.

> Either the prosecutors or the lawyers are responsible for the mistrial.

Both subjects are plural, so the verb must be plural.

> Either the prosecutors or the lawyer is responsible for the mistrial.

Since you have one plural and one singular subject, the verb agrees with the one nearer to the verb. In this case, it's the singular noun, "lawyer."

One additional guideline needs to be added to the above:

- The correlative conjunctions are "locked" pairs; in other words, we don't mix "either" with "nor" or "neither" with "or."

One of the quirky characteristics of the English language, either SWAE or colloquial English, is that past tense verbs don't change form as often as present tense verbs. For instance, in the sentences above, if you changed the present tense of the verb "know" to the past tense form, then the agreement becomes much easier.

Neither the professor nor the student knew the solution to the problem.
Neither the professor nor the students knew the solution to the problem.
Neither the professors nor the students knew the solution to the problem.

However, when you are dealing with forms of the verb "to be" or "to have," the past tense has both a plural and a singular form: "was/were" and "has/have." So in the sentences about the mistrial, you need to be a bit more careful.

Either the prosecutors or the lawyers were responsible for the mistrial.
Either the prosecutors or the lawyer was responsible for the mistrial.

The above information does not cover all the iterations of the subject/verb agreement error. There is, of course, the "echoing question" construction, represented by the sentence "She's intelligent, isn't she?" In strict comma splice application, this would be considered an error, but in this particular structure, the comma-splice error doesn't apply. Then there is the mystifying "collective noun," which can be either singular or plural depending on the context. Here is what the online site GrammarBook.com says about collective nouns: If the noun is acting as a unit, use the singular verb. Here is the sample sentence:

The team is heading for practice this afternoon.

However, if the noun indicates individual actions, then the verb should be plural.

The team are eating with their families tonight.[2]

The previous sentence is complicated by the plural pronoun, so if you decided to use the singular verb because the team is acting as a unit, then you would be stuck with a plural pronoun with no clear antecedent. The following sentence exemplifies this problem:

The team is eating with its families tonight.

There is really no "rule" that covers collective nouns, since the sense of singular or plural seems very subjective. In this case, the British have a more sensible solution. All collective nouns are considered plural since more than one person is implied. Hence, the sentences above would look like this:

The team are heading to practice this afternoon.
The team are eating with their families tonight.

Admittedly, a sentence like the following with a collective noun may seem a bit strange to American English writers:

Lakeland Community College have many interesting course offerings.

Finally, there is the special situation in which the verb seems to have two possible subjects, the choice of which is determined by the meaning the writer wishes to convey. Before this tricky structure is examined, it is necessary to review the complex sentence pattern analyzed in chapter 9. If you remember, a complex sentence has one main clause and one or more subordinate clauses. The subject-verb relationship in this pattern can cause problems, but only in one particular manifestation of this pattern: M SC C.
This is a typical sentence exhibiting this pattern:

The letter that I sent to my granddaughter was not delivered.

The subordinate clause, "that I sent to my granddaughter," is sandwiched between the subject and verb of the main clause:

Subject: "The letter"
Verb: "was . . . delivered" (the adverb "not" is not part of the verb)

The problem lurking within this pattern is represented by a sentence like this:

This is the smell of peppers that always makes me sick.

Admittedly, this is a subtle construction that requires the writer to signal meaning with the number of the verb. The question is, what is making the writer sick: the "smell" or "peppers"? If it is "peppers," then the verb should be plural:

This is the smell of peppers that always make me sick.

If the meaning is the "smell," then the verb is singular:

This is the smell of peppers that always makes me sick.

What makes this construction tricky and subtle is that the clause marker "that" is a relative pronoun, a category of pronouns that introduces subordinate clauses that are functioning like adjectives. In each of the sentences above, the clause marker/relative pronoun "that" modifies a word, but in each sentence the word it modifies is different. Whether the modified word is singular or plural, the pronoun "that" stays the same.

In summary, the subject-verb agreement "rules" aren't always logical or even consistent. If you are in doubt, consult the numerous grammar books, stylebooks, or websites for guidance. Or, even better, you can re-read this chapter!

ESSENTIAL IDEAS IN THIS CHAPTER

- No other characteristic of SWAE sentences seems to cause more problems for novice SWAE writers than the subject-verb relationship.
- Reed-Kellogg sentence diagramming seems to make sentence analysis too complicated.
- The major characteristic of the subject-verb relationship is agreement.
- Agreement states that the subject of the clause must agree in number with the verb of the clause.
- The concept of agreement is a fascinating and complex process that occurs in most languages.
- Even though English is classified as an analytical language, there are inflectional characteristics of English.
- The children's book *That Pesky S: A Jed Simon Grammar Mystery* is about the role that the letter "s" plays in the inflectional structure of English.
- The error in the sentence "The cost of all the groceries are much more than I can afford" is dependent on the writer's understanding of the concept of embedding.

- The sentence error in "Each of the students were on the bus" is a combination of embedding and pronoun usage.
- Many indefinite pronouns take singular verbs.
- One of the quirky characteristics of the English language is that past tense verbs don't show as much inflectional change as present tense verbs.

NOTES

1. Philip Skerry and Amelia Babin Horvat, *That Pesky S: A Jed Simon Grammar Mystery* (Cleveland: Sidestreet Press, 2018).

2. "Subject and Verb Agreement with Collective Nouns," GrammarBook.com, https://data.grammarbook.com/blog/singular-vs-plural/subject-and-verb-agreement-with-collective-nouns/ (accessed October 2, 2017).

Thirteen

Agreement II

Pronouns

Pronouns are essential elements of SWAE and the other dialects of English. Of all the parts of speech, with the exception of verbs, pronouns show the most inflectional forms. In addition, there are more categories of pronouns than there are for the other parts of speech. For review, here are some of the categories discussed in previous chapters.

1. Verbs: action transitive, action intransitive, linking, "to be"
2. Conjunctions: subordinate, coordinating, correlative
3. Clauses: main and subordinate (noun, adjective, adverb)
4. Phrases: prepositional, appositive, verb, participial (present and past), gerund, infinitive
5. Nouns: common and proper

This is not an exhaustive list, but it gives you an idea of the complex elements that go into creating correct SWAE sentences and fixing errors that occur in the application of these elements. You've seen the indefinite pronoun category in the discussion of subject-verb agreement errors: each, everybody, nobody, someone, one, most, all, everything, etc. As you discovered, most of these indefinite pronouns are singular and thus take singular verbs.

Just as subjects and verbs agree, so too do pronouns and their antecedents. Look at this sentence with a pronoun agreement error and see where the error occurs and how to fix it.

> The students file into the classroom, and then each gets a copy of their grades.

This is a compound sentence with this pattern: MC, cc MC. Since there are two clauses, there are two subject-verb relationships.

In the first clause, the subject is "students," and the verb is "file." The agreement is correct since the subject is plural, as is the verb. The second clause also has correct agreement; the subject is the singular indefinite pronoun "each," so the verb is singular as well, "gets." So far, so good.

Now look more closely at the sentence to examine the pronoun relationship. Can you spot two pronouns, one indefinite—"each"—and another one—"their"—which is categorized as a personal pronoun? The pronoun "their" is plural, and the antecedent is the indefinite pronoun "each." Remember that "antecedent" is a fancy term for the word that a pronoun refers to. The personal pronoun "each" is the antecedent that "their" refers to. You have learned that "each" is singular, and "their" is plural. So there is a glitch in the agreement. How do you fix it?

You can try to make "their" agree with "each" by substituting a singular personal pronoun. Many years ago, English students would have a relatively easy and automatic substitution. They would have simply used the personal pronoun "his" to make the sentence read:

> The students file into the classroom, and then each gets a copy of his grades.

In the conventions of SWAE that held forth before the 1960s, it was common—and correct—practice for one to use the masculine singular pronoun when the gender of the antecedent was not known. However, if the sentence read, "The girls file into the classroom, and then each gets a copy of her grades," then the feminine singular would be used because the gender of the antecedent is known. The same would be true if we substituted "boys" for "girls": the pronoun would then be "his."

In the decades following the 1960s, however, conventions that seemed to favor the male gender over the female began to be questioned, and writers were faced with finding pronouns that did not reflect "gender bias." Hence, the "his/her" or "his or her" combination began to be used.

The following are a few ways to correct the pronoun/antecedent errors in the sample sentence above.

> The students file into the classroom, and then they get a copy of their grades.

In this sentence, all the nouns and pronouns were made plural to avoid the pronoun error.

> The students file into the classroom, and then each gets a copy of his or her grades.

In this correction, the "his or her" (or "his/her") construction makes agreement with the singular "each." Currently, however, since the very basis of gender identification is being questioned, there are suggestions for a whole new category of personal pronouns, which, if you remember, are listed in the introduction. Here is the correction using the suggested pronouns from this new category:

> The students file into the classroom, and each gets a copy of zir grades.

This is a radical solution to the problem that would most likely not be found in the dictionary or in the various handbooks and stylebooks available to writers. However, novice SWAE writers should stick to a more traditional solution to the error. One unusual example of the social dimension of language as it reflects gender bias is this brief piece from the weekly magazine *The Week*, under the heading "Only in America":

> Under a proposed new policy, University of Minnesota students and faculty could be expelled or fired if they refer to someone by the wrong pronoun. The policy would allow all university members to choose their own pronouns—including "she," "he," "they," and "ze"—and calls for "appropriate" penalties, up to expulsion and dismissal, for those who fail to go along.[1]

Talk about grammar police!

The introduction discussed the following sentence as an example of a gray area of usage: "The captain asked that everybody on the boat wear their lifejackets." Many writers would leave this sentence as is even though there is an error in pronoun/antecedent agreement. Some writers would not leave this sentence as it stands. Rather, they would change "everybody" to "all passengers" so that "their" would have a plural antecedent. Remember that SWAE usually presents alternatives to problems in sentence construction.

Kory Stamper's delightful book *Word by Word: The Secret Life of Dictionaries* offers another point of view on this usage. Kory Stamper is a lexicographer—a dictionary writer—for Merriam-Webster, the publisher of the authoritative *Webster's Third New International Dictionary of the English Language*. In the preface to her book, Stamper notes:

> Throughout this book, I will be using the singular "their" in place of the gender-neutral "his" or the awkward "his or her" when the gender of the referent isn't known. I know some people think this is controversial, but this usage goes back to the fourteenth century. Better writers than I have used the singular "their" or "they," and the language has not fallen all to hell.

This note is in reference to the following sentence from the preface, relating to an Irish usage of the word "cat" to describe bad weather: "Yet every part of a dictionary definition is crafted by a person sitting in an office, their* eyes squeezed shut as they consider how best to describe, concisely and accurately, that weather meaning of the word 'cat.'"²

Stamper felt it necessary to employ the asterisk and the note because she knew that readers would raise their collective eyebrows over the lack of agreement between "person" and "their." It would be tough to argue with Stamper, however, about this particular usage since she has at her command a vast knowledge of the history of words and their various uses, including agreement.

In the previous chapter, I promised to comment on the differences between American and British standard usage. One area is pronoun case and agreement. The following sentence appears in Oxford-educated Yuval Noah Harari's seminal work, *Homo Deus: A Brief History of Tomorrow*: "Indeed, in some fields, the Facebook algorithm did better than the person themself."³ To American readers, "themself" looks like nonstandard usage. In addition, it is intended to agree with the singular noun "person."

However, in relation to "themself" in British and World English, the Oxford Dictionaries website states that it can be "used instead of 'himself' or 'herself' to refer to a person of unspecified sex." In SWAE, "themself" would be considered a nonstandard reflexive form of the third-person pronoun—"himself," "herself," "themselves." The Oxford website provides the following explanation for the seemingly nonstandard usage: "The singular form of themselves, first recorded in the fourteenth century, has re-emerged in recent years corresponding to the singular gender-neutral use of they."⁴

To close this chapter, here is a paragraph from the "Essay" section of the *New York Times Book Review* titled "How to Live with Critics (Whether You're an Artist or the President)." This segment illustrates several different ways that the writer, Adam Kirsch, tries to adhere to the pronoun agreement "rules" of SWAE as well as to reflect current social dimensions of language. Referring to the title of his essay, Kirsch writes:

> There is no way to stifle this question, which is the foundation of all criticism. Every reader or viewer or listener asks it, whether they want to or not. A critic is just a reader or viewer or listener who makes the question explicit and tries to answer it publicly, for the benefit of other potential readers or viewers or listeners. In doing so, she operates on the assumption that the audience for a work, the recipient of a gift, is entitled to make a judgment on its worth. The realm of judgment is plural. Everyone brings his or her own values and standards to the work of judging. This means that it is also, essentially, democratic. No canon of taste or critical authority can compel people to like what they don't like.⁵

Before you analyze the pronoun-antecedent agreement in this passage, you need to realize that the *New York Times* is the "newspaper of record" for events that take place in the United States and around the world. As such, the paper adheres to the strictest application of the rules of SWAE, while at the same time it must observe the guidelines contained in *The New York Times Manual of Style and Usage*, the newspaper's official style manual. Your analysis of the passage can begin with the second sentence of the piece. But before you start, you should take a minute or two to examine the sentence and come up with your own analysis.

If you are back, start with the sentence "Every reader or viewer or listener asks it, whether they want to or not." The word "every" is a type of adjective called a "determiner," the function of which is to describe or limit a noun. The adjective "every" always modifies a singular noun, so the three nouns in the sentence are singular: "reader," "viewer," and "listener." If you remember the discussion of coordinating conjunctions in chapter 8, you'll recall the acronym FANBOYS (for, and, nor, but, or, yet, so). So the word "or" connects or conjoins the three nouns that it modifies (no need to repeat the adjective for every word).

If you remember the chapter on agreement, you'll remember that the conjunction "and" makes the subject plural, but the conjunction "or" keeps the subjects singular. Hence, in the sentence that you're analyzing, the nouns "reader," "viewer," and "listener" are all subjects, but the verb "asks" is singular, in keeping with the rule about "or." The problem arises with the second clause, the subordinate clause beginning with the clause marker "whether." In that clause, you have the plural personal pronoun "they," the antecedents of which are three singular nouns. Do you see the dilemma here?

The guideline is clear about pronouns agreeing in number with the word they refer back to. So what if there are three words and they are all singular? The sentence would be confusing if the writer tried to make the pronoun singular: "Every reader, listener, or viewer asks it, whether he wants to or not," or "whether she wants to or not."

Notice that if you try either of these solutions—or even "whether he or she wants to or not"—you must make the verb singular: "wants." So the writer opts for a plural pronoun for clarity. There's even a logic to the choice since there are three noun antecedents, even if they are connected by a conjunction that keeps them separate subjects. Of course, the writer could have written a differently worded sentence because, as noted before, SWAE always provides grammatical alternatives for expressing ideas.

Continuing with the analysis, you'll notice that the next sentence attempts to avoid the sex bias of the masculine pronoun "he" by using the feminine pronoun "she": "In doing so, she operates on the assumption that the audience for a work, the recipient of a gift, is entitled to make a judgment on its worth." Another choice the author makes is to consider the noun "audience" as a collective singular and thus to choose a singular verb to go with it, "is."

A quick review is necessary before you continue your analysis: the noun "audience" is the subject of the subordinate clause "that the audience for a work, the recipient of a gift, is entitled to make a judgment on its worth," and the word group "the recipient of a gift" is an appositive phrase renaming the noun "audience," with a prepositional phrase embedded within it, "of a gift." At this stage in your understanding of SWAE, you are hopefully beginning to see how the elements of a sentence work together to convey meaning within a network of "rules" of usage.

The sixth sentence of the passage, "Everyone brings his or her own values and standards to the work of judging," represents an awareness of the singular number of the pronoun "everyone" and the need to avoid sex bias in the personal pronoun.

The last sentence of the piece, "No canon of taste or critical authority can compel people to like what they don't like," is a conventional solution to the agreement criterion: "people" is plural, so the pronoun is made plural so that it agrees with its antecedent, "they."

Hopefully this analysis has helped you see how a professional writer navigates the tricky waters of SWAE, sticking to some traditional rules of usage but trying to recognize that even SWAE changes.

ESSENTIAL IDEAS IN THIS CHAPTER

- Next to verbs, pronouns show the most inflection forms of all the parts of speech.
- Just as subjects and verbs agree, so too do pronouns and their antecedents.
- An antecedent is a fancy term for the word that a pronoun refers to.
- Personal pronouns reflect changes in gender identification.
- SWAE writers should be sensitive to sex bias in the use of pronouns.

NOTES

1. "Only in America," *The Week*, August 10, 2018, 6.
2. Kory Stamper, *Word by Word: The Secret Life of Dictionaries* (New York: Pantheon Books, 2017), xii.
3. Yuval Noah Harari, *Homo Deus: A Brief History of Tomorrow* (New York: Harper Perennial, 2017), 345.
4. "Themselves," Oxford Dictionaries website, https://www.lexico.com/definition/themselves (accessed October 15, 2017).
5. Adam Kirsch, "How to Live with Critics (Whether You're an Artist or the President)," *New York Times*, June 14, 2017, https://www.nytimes.com/2017/06/14/books/review/how-to-live-with-critics.html (accessed October 15, 2017).

Fourteen

Additional Pronoun Problems

In the previous chapter, pronoun-antecedent agreement problems were examined in some detail. In this chapter, you'll look at some characteristics of pronouns that lead to other errors in sentence construction. The previous chapter claimed that pronouns have more categories than any other part of speech and that, next to verbs, they show the most inflection.

The category of personal pronouns is a good way to illustrate inflectional forms. Below is a list of functional forms that these pronouns exhibit. Remember that in chapter 4 there was a distinction made between "parts-of-speech" grammar and functional grammar. The part of speech known as a noun can function as a subject, a direct object, an indirect object, and an object of a preposition. A noun can also function as a possessive with an apostrophe and an "s" in the appropriate position (boy's room—boys' room).

Here are the functional forms for personal pronouns. Most of them will sound familiar, but one might be new. English and language arts teachers call these forms "pronoun cases," a term derived from the study of Latin grammar.

- Subject
- Object (Direct, Indirect, Object of Preposition)
- Possessive
- Reflexive/Intensive

The following paragraphs list the various forms that personal pronouns take as they fulfill their functions. The forms for the first-person pronoun will be listed, followed by illustrations with sample sentences.

- Subject: I
- Object (Direct, Indirect, Object of Preposition): me
- Possessive: my, mine
- Reflexive/Intensive: myself

1. Subject

    I gave the last piece of cake to Sara Jane.
    It was I who sent the anonymous letter.

2. Direct Object

    The baseball hit me just above the knee.

3. Indirect Object

    Juan's cousin gave me the last piece of cake.

4. Object of Preposition

    The argument was between Bob and me.

5. Possessive

    That wreck used to be my car.
    That wreck used to be mine.

6. Reflexive/Intensive

    I hurt myself while lifting weights.
    The test was so hard that I, myself, flunked it.

Some of these sentences may need some discussion. The first one, the subject, is fairly straightforward. However, the following forms appears in colloquial (conversational or slang) English: "Me and Roberta went to the baseball game" and "Roberta and me went to the baseball game." If you keep in mind the functional forms, you will avoid this in SWAE, since the form "me" is the object form. In the sentence "It was I who sent the anonymous letter," the use of the subject form "I" might seem strange, but it is correct in SWAE terms because "to be" verbs do not take objects.

At this point, you might want to review clause classifications in chapter 5. The clause "It was I" represents this pattern: Subject–"to be" verb–predicate nominative ("nominative" means "subject"). The direct object example—"The baseball hit me just above the knee"—is a form of this clause classification: subject–transitive verb–direct object. The indirect object sentence—"Juan's cousin gave me the last piece of cake"—is a form of this clause pattern: subject–transitive verb–indirect object–direct object. The indirect object is "me," and the direct object is "piece."

When it comes to the object of the preposition, you need to remember the different types of phrases. The prepositional phrase is composed of a preposition and an object of the preposition, which is usually the last word of the phrase. In the sample sentence, there are actually two objects of the preposition: "Bob" and "me." The noun "Bob" does *not* undergo inflectional change when it goes from subject to object, but the pronoun does: "I" to "me."

The last two forms of pronouns are the possessive and the reflexive/intensive. These also require some explanation. The possessive form comes in two shapes: the personal pronoun "mine" and the pronominal adjective "my." Don't be put off by the terminology; SWAE, like other cultural forms and disciplines, has its own vocabulary, much of it derived from Latin. The term "pronominal" means derived from or pertaining to a pronoun.

In the sample sentence "That wreck used to be my car," the pronoun "my" is functioning as an adjective modifying the noun "car." When you identify elements of SWAE sentences, you may run across words that cross the barrier between parts of speech and functional elements. So the word "my" is classified in parts-of-speech grammar as a pronoun, but in functional terms, it is an adjective since it modifies a noun. The concept of modification will be addressed in the next chapter.

The reflexive/intensive pronoun form is used when the action of the verb refers back to the subject. In the sentence "I hurt myself while lifting weights," the reflexive is needed to clarify the meaning of the sentence. If you used the object form of the pronoun, the sentence would be confusing—"I hurt me while lifting weights."

When the pronoun does not receive the action of the verb but rather intensifies or emphasizes another noun or pronoun, the pronoun is called "intensive." In the sample sentence, the intensive pronoun "myself" gives special emphasis to the pronoun "I." What the sentence says is that the difficulty of the test has special meaning for the speaker. Perhaps the "I" who is taking the test is a teacher or someone who is expected to pass the test. Notice how different the sentence would be if you used just the pronoun "I" without the intensifier: "The test was so hard that I flunked it."

Below is a list of the subject forms of the other personal pronouns with some sample sentences.

Subject Forms of Personal Pronouns

You
He
She
It
We
You (plural)
They

Sample Sentences

- You had to be a genius to pass that test.
- He gave Jackie the answers to the test questions.
- She compared her answers with those of her friend.
- The spider climbed up the wall, and then it began to spin a web.
- We watched in fascination as the spider did its work.
- The teacher said to the students, "Now that you have the test booklets, you may begin."
- They all sat down and began to work on the test.

Object Forms of Personal Pronouns

Me
You
Him
Her
It
Us
You (plural)
Them

Sample Sentences

- Between you and me, I think Jackie's new hairstyle looks terrible.
- I realize that the argument is between you and Bob.
- The argument was between him and Bob.
- The argument was between her and Bob.
- Before the cat could run into the garage, I grabbed it.
- The argument is between them and us.
- The argument is between you and Bob.

In the sample sentences above, the prepositional phrase structure is used to demonstrate the correct object form of the personal pronouns. For some reason, many writers who should know better insist on using the subject form of the pronoun in prepositional phrases. For example, some writers would write the first sentence this way: "Between you and I, I think Jackie's new hairstyle looks terrible." This usage is common in colloquial English (everyday spoken English), but it should be avoided in SWAE.

At this point, a slight digression is necessary to address a problem that occurs with relative pronouns, those words that frequently introduce subordinate clauses acting as adjectives. Look at these sentences:

The person who you brought to the concert hated the music.
The writer whom just won the prize has been nominated many times before.

Did you see anything wrong with these sentences? There are errors, and these occur because of the confusion surrounding the "who/whom" distinction.

The letter "m" at the end of "whom" is a leftover from the Latin ending for the object form. Some writers claim that this distinction is slowly disappearing from formal usage, and many of them welcome this development, since they claim that most people have little understanding of the different forms. This may be true, but for now, SWAE writers should try to use the forms correctly.

Here is a little tip to help students master this mystifying usage: the case of "who" or "whom" depends on its function in its own clause. In the above sentences, you have a typical complex sentence pattern: M SC C, with the subordinate clause sandwiched between the subject and verb of the main clause. Can you follow some of the guidelines provided in previous chapters to help you understand the problem? If you remember, a clause has a subject-verb relationship. If you have two clauses, then you have two subject-verb relationships.

In the first sentence, the main clause is "The person . . . hated the music." The sandwiched subordinate clause functions as an adjective modifying the subject of the main clause, "The person." In order to find the subject of a verb, you must first find the verb and then ask, "Who or what . . . ?" So, in the subordinate clause, the verb is "brought," and if you ask, "Who or what brought?" then the answer is "you." If the clause has the subject-verb transitive–direct object form, then you ask of the verb, "Brought whom or what?" and the answer is the direct object.

In the first sentence, then, if the subject is "you," then the object is "who," but the pronoun "who" is in the wrong case: it should be "whom." In the second sentence, the "whom" is incorrect because it is the subject of the clause: "Who or what won the prize?" The answer is "who," not "whom." If all of this seems too complicated, then you can always default to the nongendered and uninflected adjective "that":

The person that you brought to the concert hated the music.
The person that won the prize has been nominated many times before.

Is this use of "that" considered standard usage? Well, you'll probably get different answers, depending on the "rules of the game" of the organization.

Possessive Forms of Personal Pronouns

My, Mine
Your, Yours
His
Her, Hers
Its
Our, Ours
Your, Yours
Their, Theirs

Sample Sentences

- This is my house. The house is mine.
- Is this your car? Is this yours?
- The party was at his house.
- This is her car. This is hers.
- The cat hurt its paw.
- This is our car. The car is ours.
- Is this your car? Is it yours?
- This is their car. This is theirs.

There are some important points to make about the above sentences. Similar patterns and short sentences have been used to illustrate the major points. Perhaps the most common error associated with the possessive pronouns is with the form ending in "s": yours (singular and plural), hers, its, ours, and theirs. It is tempting to use the apostrophe with the possessive pronouns because you usually use the apostrophe to show possession. For example, if you substitute a noun for the pronoun in the sentence "This is hers," you might say, "This is Caroline's."

As with many of the errors in SWAE, a problem arises when you try to apply a grammatical rule to a situation where it doesn't work. You saw this problem earlier in the comma-splice sentence involving a conjunctive adverb like "however" linking two main clauses: "We studied hard for the test, however we didn't pass it." The error occurred because the writer tried to apply the formula MC, cc MC to the formula MC; tw MC. The two correct sentences are "We studied hard for the test; however, we didn't pass it" and "We studied hard for the test, but we didn't pass it."

Here are some sentences using the possessive pronoun incorrectly:

- We didn't realize that the house was her's.
- Is this car your's?
- Theirs' was the most important contribution.

If you substitute nouns for the sentences, you can see how this error occurs:

- We didn't realize that the house was Geraldo's.
- Is this car Geraldo's?
- The lawyers' contribution was the most important.

The corrected sentences are as follows:

- We didn't realize that the house was hers.
- Is this car yours?
- Theirs was the most important contribution.

An additional apostrophe error occurs with confusion between "its" and "it's." Grammarians call these two forms "homophones," words that sound the same but have different spelling and meanings. The word "its" is a possessive personal pronoun, and it falls under the category of possessives that don't take apostrophes. The homophonous word "it's" is a contraction for "it is," with the apostrophe signaling the omission of the letter "i." No wonder writers get confused with these forms! Of course, when you speak, you don't indicate punctuation, other than pauses between clauses and items in a series, and the drop in pitch to signal the end of a sentence.

Here is a sentence for you to analyze: "It's a shame that the cat hurt it's paw." If you sense something is wrong with the it/it's usage here, you are on your way to understanding the problem. The first "its" is not the personal pronoun "its"; rather, it's (the form used correctly!) a subject pronoun "it" with the verb "is" contracted to the form "it's" = "it is." The second "it's" is not a contraction but rather the personal pronoun, which does not require an apostrophe (you wouldn't say "the cat hurt it is paw"). So, after all that, here is the corrected sentence: "It's a shame that the cat hurt its paw."

Another area of confusion is the use of the same form in the singular and plural. This is the case with "you" and "yours." In the following sentence, you have no way of knowing whether the antecedent is singular or plural: "Would you please follow me?" The meaning is different if the writer is speaking to one person or a group of people. Languages like Spanish have different forms for the pronoun equivalent to "you": "usted" (singular) and "ustedes" (plural) are two of them.

In colloquial English, this problem is solved somewhat in regional dialects. The southern "y'all" and the Pennsylvanian/West Virginian "y'uns" (or "y'ins") are forms for the plural meaning of "you." However, contemporary usage seems to be heading toward inclusivity, with "y'all" and "y'uns," or "y'ins," indicating both singular and plural. Of course, these examples refer to the informal, spoken dialects of English, but in SWAE, informal usages sometimes seep into the more formal dialect.

Reflexive/Intensive Forms of Personal Pronoun

Myself
Yourself
Himself
Herself
Itself
Ourselves
Yourselves
Themselves

Sample Sentences

- When I am nervous, I often talk to myself.
- I designed the course with so many hills that I, myself, couldn't finish the race!
- Be careful sharpening the knife so that you don't cut yourself.
- Omar hurt himself while rock climbing.
- Sarah frequently dresses herself, even though she is still recovering from surgery.
- The cat cleans itself every evening.
- We treated ourselves to an expensive bottle of wine.
- Please make yourselves comfortable.
- The players humbled themselves before the team's new coach.

Most of the sentences above don't need comments. However, there are some anomalies and frequently made errors. The anomaly is that a distinction is made between the plural and singular forms of the second-person reflexive-intensive pronouns "yourself" and "yourselves," but the same distinction isn't made with the possessive pronoun "you." The errors are a different story because they cut across colloquial and standard usage. Here are some examples:

- Bob cut hisself while shaving.
- When we are stressed, we sometimes talk to ourself.
- The guests helped theirselves to the desserts.

These usages are common in some of the regional and ethnic dialects. It would be helpful at this point to discuss the African-American dialect that linguists refer to as African-American Vernacular English (AAVE). Many of the common sentence constructions in AAVE violate SWAE rules:

- He don't know nothing.
- When he get home from work, he do nothing to help around the house.
- We be heading home soon.

When students make these kinds of errors in class, the professor usually reminds them that the English they are required to learn and use in college classes is different from the kind of English they use with their families and friends. They are also usually reminded that their colloquial dialect is perfectly appropriate for social situations they find themselves in but that formal writing requires adherence to the demands of SWAE.

ESSENTIAL IDEAS IN THIS CHAPTER

- Pronouns have more categories that any other part of speech.
- Personal pronouns exhibit different forms that are called cases.
- The major cases of the personal pronoun are subject, object, possessive, and reflexive/intensive.
- The most common error associated with personal pronouns in the possessive case is with the forms ending in "s": hers, its, ours, and theirs.
- Homophones are words that sound the same but are spelled differently.

Fifteen

Modification

At the end of the introduction, good writing is defined as "the right words in the right order." It is time now to address the second part of the definition: "the right order." As pointed out earlier, word order is a major characteristic of an analytical language like English, which depends partly on this order to make meaning in sentences. It is also important to consider the inflectional nature of many of the elements of SWAE sentences, such as, the rule about subject-verb agreement. Word order is the culprit, though, in many errors in SWAE sentences. The following are a few examples:

- Hanging on by his fingertips, the policeman rescued the burglar from the fire escape.
- Embarrassed by the many errors in her paper, the professor tried to encourage the student to revise her work.
- To improve writing, hard work is the answer.

These three sentences illustrate the "dangling modifier" error, which has been the subject of several jokes. Here is one from Eric K. Auld that is noted in the blog *Writing On*: "A dangling modifier walks into a bar. After finishing a drink, the bartender asks it to leave."[1]

Errors like these violate the rule of modification, which requires that modifiers be placed as close as possible to the words they modify. To modify means to change or alter something. A mechanic, for example, can modify an engine to give it more power, just as a lawyer can modify her appeal to the jury to come up with a verdict of not guilty. In grammatical terms, to modify means to alter or change the meaning of another sentence element.

For instance, the noun "hotel" can be modified with an adjective in these ways: old hotel, expensive hotel, abandoned hotel, modern hotel. Or it can be modified by a phrase: the hotel on the corner, the hotel with the elegant sign, the hotel on the Riviera, the hotel being remodeled, the hotel destroyed by the hurricane. It can also be modified by a clause: the hotel that burned down; the new Hilton Hotel, which recently opened.

With this information about modification, can you analyze the errors in the sentences above? In the first sentence, it is clearly *not* the policeman who is hanging by his fingertips, nor in the second sentence is the professor the embarrassed party. In the third sentence, "hard work" can't be the agent who improves writing. Here are the corrections of the modification errors:

- Hanging on by his fingertips, the burglar was rescued by the policeman.
- Embarrassed by the many errors in her paper, the student was encouraged by her professor to revise her work.
- To improve writing, one must work hard.

English teachers love to categorize errors. Under modification errors, for example, they usually would point out two kinds to their students: dangling and misplaced. Look at these two sentences.

I showed my dog to the neighbor that just had pups.
Feeling sick to my stomach, my movie date was canceled.

The first sentence illustrates the misplaced modifier error, which can usually be fixed by rearranging the word order:

I showed my dog that just had pups to the neighbor.

The other error, a "true" dangling modifier, can't be fixed by moving the sentence elements around because the introductory participial phrase (remember those?) doesn't connect grammatically to any word or words in the sentence. When students are shown this error, some maintain that the phrase is modifying the word "my" and is thus not dangling. "Nice try, but no cigar!" might be an appropriate response.

The reason that the participial phrase can't modify "my" is that "my" itself is a modifier: it is acting like an adjective modifying the noun "date." Since the participial phrase is functioning as an adjective, it can't be modified by another adjective; hence, the phrase is "dangling": it has nothing to attach to. The noun in the clause—"date"—doesn't work since that noun can't be sick to its stomach.

Perhaps a digression on the function of adjectives is in order here since adjectives are so common in writing. Grammarians classify adjectives into three categories: determiners, noun adjuncts, and true adjectives. Let's start with the last category first. A true adjective is one that can take the inflectional endings "–er" and "–est" or that can take "more" or "most" in front of it. So, for example, "tall" is an adjective since we can add the suffixes "–er" or "–est" to make "taller" or "tallest." And "interesting" is a true adjective since we can add "more" or "most" and come up with "more interesting" or "most interesting."

A noun adjunct, on the other hand, is not a true adjective, but it is functioning like an adjective. In the sample sentence above that illustrated the dangling modifier error, the noun "movie" is functioning as an adjective modifying the noun "date." The final category is determiners, those words that aren't nouns but that function like noun adjuncts since they modify nouns. For example, in this category, one finds that the possessive pronouns are frequently determiners: "my car," "your finger," "his apartment," "their money," and so on.

The interesting characteristic of these three types of adjectives is that there is a fixed order of their arrangement in sentences. When all three appear in a phrase or clause, they are always arranged in this way: determiner, true adjective, noun adjunct. Try the following experiment. Choose a determiner—for example, "his." Then find a true adjective: how about "new." Now add a noun adjunct, "clock." Then add the noun that all of these modify: "radio." Now you have: "his new clock radio."

The order is fixed: one would not (or should not!) write "his clock radio new" or "new clock his radio." The fixed arrangement of determiner–true adjective–noun adjunct–noun is a perfect example of the importance of word order in SWAE.

To return to modifier errors, if you recall the discussion of the fluid relationship between parts of speech and functional grammar, you'll remember that phrases and clauses can function as specific parts of speech. For example, the phrase "feeling sick to my stomach" is a participial phrase since it functions as an adjective. It could also be a gerund phrase if it functions like a noun: "Feeling sick to my stomach gave me a perfect excuse to cut my classes."

The gerund phrase "Feeling sick to my stomach" is the subject of the verb "gave" in the clause classification: subject–transitive verb–indirect object–direct object. (If you need a quick review of clause classifications, you can turn back to chapter 5.) The dangling modifier and misplaced modifier errors are thus best understood as the incorrect placement of modifiers.

To further complicate matters, the dangling modifier can "hide" itself within a phrase or clause. Look at the following sentence:

By studying all night, lack of sleep caused me to flunk the test.

The way this sentence is written, it seems that the "lack of sleep" was studying all night! If you analyze the structure of the sentence, you'll see that the introductory phrase is actually two phrases in one.

If you recall, this structure is referred to as an embedded phrase. The prepositional phrase is "By studying all night"; the embedded phrase is "studying all night," which is classified as a gerund phrase functioning as an object of the preposition "By." (Remember that the prepositional phrase is composed of a preposition plus its object.) What causes the error is not the prepositional phrase; rather, it is the gerund phrase "studying all night" that is the culprit.

Unlike the misplaced modifier, which usually can be fixed by rearranging the elements of the sentence, the dangling modifier requires rewriting the sentence. In rewriting the sentence above, you have two choices: leave the main clause as is and rewrite the introductory phrase, or leave the introductory phrase as is and rewrite the main clause.

Try the first choice—rewriting the introductory phrase:

Because I studied all night, lack of sleep caused me to flunk the test.

Admittedly, this is not the most elegant sentence, but it does eliminate the dangling modifier. The second choice, rewriting the main clause, produces this sentence:

By studying all night, I was so tired that I flunked the test.

It is important to remember that these corrections are just two of several different options. If you notice, the second choice results in a sentence that has significant differences from the original. In effect, a sentence was created with a different pattern: a complex sentence with the formula MCSC.

On the other hand, the first correction choice retained the pattern of the original sentence. It is a simple sentence because it has one main clause and no subordinate clauses. To emphasize, knowledge of SWAE gives you the tools to create error-free sentences or to correct sentences that have errors in them.

Finally, not only can phrases and clauses can be misplaced; individual words can be as well. Look at these sentences and see if you can identify what makes them unclear:

She lost nearly her whole deposit.
He almost won all of the money.
Talking rapidly annoys people.

Here are some questions that will help you see how the sentences might be ambiguous. In the first sentence, did she nearly lose her deposit, or did she lose nearly her whole deposit? In the second sentence, did he almost win all the money, or did he win almost all the money? And finally, is the person talking rapidly, or does his talking rapidly annoy people? Admittedly, these distinctions of meaning may seem subtle to some writers and readers, but SWAE depends on making subtle distinctions to clarify meaning.

ESSENTIAL IDEAS IN THIS CHAPTER

- Word order is the major characteristic of an analytical language like English.
- Errors in word order are called modification errors.
- The two major types of modification errors are the misplaced modifier and the dangling modifier.
- The rule of modification requires that modifiers be placed as close as possible to the words they modify.
- Grammarians classify adjectives into three categories: determiners, noun adjuncts, and true adjectives.
- Adjectives can also be involved in modification errors.

NOTE

1. Eric K. Auld, "A Joke Worth Sharing," *Writing On* (blog), November 8, 2011, https://writerlingearthling.blogspot.com.

Sixteen

Punctuation

You knew that you would have to contend with this dreaded topic—"dreaded" because no other aspect of SWAE causes more vexation than punctuation! Those little black marks—periods, commas, semicolons, apostrophes, hyphens, dashes, parentheses, ellipses—give both novice and veteran writers severe headaches. But punctuation is not just those things: it also pertains to the spacing of words, sentences, and paragraphs and to the layout of text in both hard copy and electronic formats.

As the eminent language scholar David Crystal claims in his book *Making a Point: The Persnickety Story of English Punctuation*, the space between words is the most basic form of punctuation. He offers this example: "therapistsneedspecialtreatment." Crystal says of this: "we need to know if this is a text about sex crimes or about speech pathology before we can correctly read it aloud." If we space it this way—"the rapists need special treatment"—then it is about sex crimes; but if we space it another way—"therapists need special treatment"—then it is about speech pathology or psychological counseling.[1]

You will hopefully be relieved to find out that you are not going through the ins and outs of every type of punctuation. You can easily consult textbooks or websites to get most of the answers to punctuation questions. For example, the Online Writing Lab at Purdue University—the OWL—provides comprehensive information about punctuating SWAE texts (https://owl.english.purdue.edu/owl/). For the purposes of this book, punctuation will be reviewed as it pertains to the sentence information in the previous chapters.

It might help if you keep in mind David Crystal's two classifications of punctuation: the semantic and the pragmatic. The semantic—the meaning of words and sentences—can be exemplified by the title of Lynne Truss's *Eats, Shoots and Leaves: The Zero Tolerance Approach to Punctuation*. Truss's book announces its credo in the title: "Zero Tolerance." Truss is a prescriptivist who insists on strict adherence to the punctuation "rules" of SWAE. Her title illustrates her point; there's semantic confusion if you leave the comma in the title, which refers to the eating habits of the panda bear. If we are referring to its foraging habits, the panda eats shoots and leaves; however, if the panda eats, shoots, and leaves, the text is referring to the actions of a hungry bank-robber Panda![2]

The pragmatic—or practical—classification refers to punctuation decisions that don't necessarily affect meaning. One example is called the Oxford comma, or serial comma, best illustrated by the following sentence:

> DeSean picked up his tuxedo, drove to his fiancée's house, and tried the tuxedo on.

The comma before the "and" is the Oxford comma, named for the punctuation standard promulgated by the editors at Oxford University Press. The sentence could be written in this way without altering the meaning:

> DeSean picked up his tuxedo, drove to his fiancée's house and tried the tuxedo on.

Promoters of the Oxford comma are quick to point out, however, that the punctuation is not always optional. As an example, on March 16, 2017, the *New York Times Online* carried an article with the title "Lack of Oxford Comma Could Cost Maine Company Millions in Overtime Dispute." The article describes an appeals court case that hinged on the omission of a comma in a list of overtime rules that exempted certain job categories from overtime pay. The court found that the omission of a comma in the overtime rules prevented employees from receiving overtime pay. The court ruled that the company owed $10 million to its employees.[3] That was quite an expensive punctuation decision!

An additional punctuation decision that can affect meaning occurs in the complex sentence pattern that was discussed in a previous chapter: M SC C. The subordinate clause is sandwiched between the subject and verb of the main clause. The most common clause markers for this pattern are "that" and "which." The punctuation "rule" that covers these conjunctions involves the use of a comma before the conjunction. Look at a few examples:

> The Buick Regal, which is like a sports car, was my birthday present to myself.
> The automobile that is most like a sports car is the Buick Regal.

In the first sentence, the clause beginning with "which" is referred to as a nonrestrictive clause since it is not necessary to the identification of the words that it follows, "Buick Regal." Nonrestrictive clauses are set off by commas. The second sentence, however, is different because the clause beginning with "that" is necessary to the meaning of "automobile." Restrictive clauses are not set off by commas.

Luckily, the punctuation decisions that you have to make won't necessarily cost you a fortune—unless you are drafting laws! How does punctuation tie in with the material in the previous chapters? Begin with the Big Three errors, which are described in chapter 11: comma splice, fused sentence, and fragment. (Notice the Oxford comma in the previous sentence?) In effect, the first two are really punctuation errors that fall into that murky area between David Crystal's pragmatic and semantic categories. For example, if you write "Alfred Hitchcock made over fifty films, however he never won an Academy Award for Best Picture or Best Director," you've committed a comma splice, which can be fixed in several different ways, all described in chapter 11. If you attempt to correct the error by omitting the comma, you make another error: the fused sentence—"Alfred Hitchcock made over fifty films however he never won an Academy Award for Best Picture or Best Director."

The above errors do not necessarily affect meaning since the sentences are understandable even with the errors. However, a SWAE writer doesn't really have the same kind of choice that she has with the Oxford comma, since almost all users of SWAE, both editors and writers, would consider these to be major errors.

The fragment error can also be called a punctuation error, but that doesn't tell the whole story because a fragment lacks a main clause. Consider the following sentences: "Walking in the rain without an umbrella. I decided to hail a cab." You can correct this error in several ways; the simplest is to replace the period with a comma: "Walking in the rain without an umbrella, I decided to hail a cab." Or you can change the opening participial phrase into a subordinate clause: "While I was walking in the rain without an umbrella, I decided to hail a cab." Either way, you have to add a comma after the participial phrase and the subordinate clause. These are semantic errors because they violate very basic punctuation "rules" of SWAE.

Chapter 11 also covers several ways of correcting the comma splice and fused sentence errors. Below is a list of the formulas for a quick review:

MC. MC
MC; MC
MC, cc MC
MC; tw, MC
SC, MC or MC SC

Two of the formulas listed above contain commas as part of their punctuation patterns. The Oxford comma that was discussed above is only one of the punctuation decisions that writers of SWAE face. Most English teachers would offer to students the following bit of wisdom about commas: "When in doubt, leave them out." In regard to punctuation advice, David Crystal makes the point that contemporary practice eschews (good SWAE vocabulary!) over-punctuating texts.[4]

That does not mean, however, that writers can ignore punctuation altogether. Remember the two characteristics of SWAE that were discussed in chapter 2: it is rule-bound, and it is conservative. As a way of summing up, a modification to the statement made above—that punctuation would be dealt with only as it related to sentence construction and correction—needs to be made.

The punctuation mark that rivals the comma as a hazard for SWAE writers is the apostrophe. Lynne Truss, the author of *Eats, Shoots and Leaves*, has also written a punctuation book for children with the delightful title *Girl's Like Spaghetti: Why, You Can't Manage without Apostrophes!*[5] Truss's book is a hilarious guide to the complexities of apostrophe usage, for both children and adults. Another humorous book on punctuation and spelling problems is *The Great Typo Hunt: Two Friends Changing the World, One Correction at a Time*, by Jeff Deck and Benjamin D. Herson.[6]

Both of these books inspired this author to write a children's book with a grammar and punctuation angle: *That Pesky S: A Jed Simon Grammar Mystery*. The coauthor is the author's granddaughter, Amelia Babin Horvat, who also acted as adviser on the world of middle-grade kids. One section of the book deals with the apostrophe. Jed's dad, Mr. Simon, a language arts teacher at his school, is always giving Jed little lessons on English usage. In one part of the story, Jed is trying to figure out what is wrong with the following sentence that his dad has given him as a challenge: "How many boys are in the boys room?" In trying to discover the error in the sentence, he remembers a lesson on apostrophe usage that his teacher, Miss Robbins, presented to the class:

> I remember Miss Robbins, my fifth-grade teacher, writing on the blackboard what she called, "the sure-fire way to punctuate possessive nouns." She put a sentence on the board: "The policeman retrieved the womans hat." Miss Robbins then showed us how to figure out where to put the apostrophe by using this formula: "The _____ of or belonging to the _____." She said that if the word in the second space does not end in an "s," we should put in an apostrophe and then an "s." But if the word ended in an "s," we should put the apostrophe after the "s."
>
> So for the sentence she wrote on the board, the class worked it out this way: "The hat of or belonging to the woman." Since the word "woman" did not end in an "s," we figured out that the word "womans" needed an apostrophe between the "n" and the "s." I thought this was pretty cool at the time, and now I tried to apply Miss Robbins' formula to dad's sentence. But

there was a problem when I put it into the formula because I couldn't tell if the room belonged to one boy or more than one. I figured out that my dad had left off the apostrophe so that I couldn't figure it out.

It was the "s" that was causing the problem! Now I saw why it was pesky! I wrote underneath dad's sentence, "I can't tell if the room belongs to one boy or more than one. If it's one boy, the apostrophe goes between the 'y' and the 's'; if it's more than one boy, the apostrophe goes after the 's.'" I made sure that I used a semicolon in the sentence so that dad could tell I knew how to use it. The whole family got a punctuation lesson after we decided (actually just dad) to call our dog "semicolon."[7]

Perhaps if all writers had dads like Mr. Simon, they wouldn't have to worry about adhering to the rules of the game!

As a final note, you may find apostrophe usage in unexpected places. In an episode of the TNT series *Murder in the First*, a suicide note with the word "shouldn't've" becomes a clue to the identity of the writer. The apostrophes lead the detectives to conclude that the suicide is actually a murder.[8]

Here's hoping that your apostrophe usage is not a matter of life and death!

ESSENTIAL IDEAS IN THIS CHAPTER

- No other aspect of SWAE causes more vexation than punctuation.
- According to language scholar David Crystal, the space between words is the most basic form of punctuation.
- David Crystal divides punctuation into the semantic and the pragmatic.
- The semantic refers to punctuation that affects meaning in sentences.
- The pragmatic refers to punctuation that doesn't necessarily affect meaning.
- Lynne Truss's book titled *Eats, Shoots and Leaves: The Zero Tolerance Approach to Punctuation* is an example of semantic punctuation.
- The Oxford comma is an example of pragmatic punctuation.
- In a sense, the "Big Three" comma splice and fused sentence are punctuation errors.
- The fragment can also be called a punctuation error.

NOTES

1. David Crystal, *Making a Point: The Persnickety Story of English Punctuation* (New York: St. Martin's Press, 2015), 5.

2. Lynne Truss, *Eats, Shoots and Leaves: The Zero Tolerance Approach to Punctuation* (New York: Gotham, 2003).

3. "Lack of Oxford Comma Could Cost Maine Company Millions in Overtime Dispute," *New York Times Online*, March 16, 2017, https://www.nytimes.com/2017/03/16/us/oxford-comma-lawsuit.html (accessed December 2, 2017).

4. Crystal, *Making a Point*, 6.

5. Lynne Truss, *Girl's Like Spaghetti: Why, You Can't Manage without Apostrophes!* (New York: G. P. Putnam, 2007).

6. Jeff Deck and Benjamin D. Herson, *The Great Typo Hunt: Two Friends Changing the World, One Correction at a Time* (New York: Broadway Books, 2011).

7. Philip Skerry and Amelia Babin Horvat, *That Pesky S: A Jed Simon Grammar Mystery* (Cleveland: Sidestreet Press, 2018), 86–88.

8. Steven Bochco, *Murder in the First*, Season 2, TNT.

Seventeen

"Form Is the Shape of Content"

The quotation in the chapter title is from the twentieth-century Russian-born American artist Ben Shahn. In many ways, SWAE is primarily about the form of writing, the structure of SWAE sentences. However, these sentences are about something, and that is where content comes in. Essentially form and content work hand in glove to create meaning. Whether you are writing an essay for an English class, preparing a manuscript for publication, or formulating chart notes in a hospital setting, you have an obligation to present your content in a responsible and honest way.

Discussed in chapter 1 is the importance of academic honesty, of being scrupulously careful in attributing credit to any source you use. For example, if you happened to have the quotation from Ben Shahn as part of your store of common knowledge, you would not have to document it. In some ways, the quotation has become part of our cultural heritage. However, if you did research on the source of this quotation, you would need to document it. Here is an example: Ben Shahn used the statement in a series of lectures that he delivered at Harvard University as part of the Charles Eliot Norton lecture series in 1956–1957. Shahn's lectures were later turned into a book titled *The Shape of Content*, published in 1957.[1] Since you discovered this additional information in a source, you must document it. *The Chicago Manual of Style* format for documenting electronic sources is used in the citation in the notes section.

The Chicago Manual of Style format is only one of several different formats. Most of the time, your teacher or an organization that you are writing for will stipulate a format for you to use. Most English teachers would stipulate to their students that the preferred format for documenting sources is that of the Modern Language Association (MLA). Here, then, is the in-text MLA citation for the source of the Shahn information: ("The Shape of Content by Ben Shahn," www.kirkusreviews.com/book-reviews/ben-shahn-3/the-shape-of-content-2).

The remainder of this chapter will focus on one type of information that will enhance your knowledge of the English language and that will help you as a SWAE writer. Latin was once a crucial part of school curricula that college-bound students were required to master. This is no longer the case. Chapter 2 pointed out that conservatism is one of the major characteristics of SWAE. In other words, SWAE is slow to change and frequently looks to past usage to create many of the rules of the game.

As an example of this look to the past, a website with an odd-sounding name points out the importance of Latin as a trait in many texts written in SWAE. Here is an excerpt from the Art of Manliness:

> From the Middle Ages until about the middle of the twentieth century, Latin was a central part of a man's schooling in the West. Along with logic and rhetoric, grammar (as Latin was then known) was included as part of the Trivium—the foundation of a medieval liberal arts education. From Latin, all scholarship flowed and it was truly the gateway to the life of the mind, as the bulk of scientific, religious, legal, and philosophical literature was written in the language until about the sixteenth century. To immerse oneself in classical and humanistic studies, Latin was a must.[2]

For those writers and scholars who studied Latin as part of their schooling, the disappearance of Latin from school curricula in the 1960s was a tragic mistake. In the previous decades, students in college or on an academic track had to take Latin as a basic part of the curriculum. Later in the 1960s, Latin was dropped from the required courses. There are many reasons why this change took place, but an important one was the belief—wrongly held, many believe—that Latin was a dead language and thus irrelevant in a modern education. The irony in this momentous change is that this "dead language" can teach you quite a bit about the living language of English.

Since many of the texts that you will read reflect traditional SWAE values, you are likely to run across Latin words and phrases, and perhaps you will be required to learn them as part of your education or your profession. Here, for example, is an excerpt from an article titled "Latin in Legal Writing: An Inquiry into the Use of Latin in the Modern Legal World," which appeared in the *Boston College Law Review* in 1998:

> Considering the former central position of Latin in many areas of European life, its importance in American legal language of earlier centuries is unsurprising. What is of interest is that Latin, at the end of the twentieth century, continues to exist in legal discourse. So, for example, first year law students still encounter Latin phrases in their classes. Judges still use Latin in their decisions. *Black's Law Dictionary* still begins with a Latin pronunciation section. Latin may be down but it is not yet out.[3]

So if you are considering a legal education, you will need to know some Latin. In the article from Art of Manliness mentioned above, the authors point out two other advantages to knowing Latin besides its use for a legal education:

1. Knowing Latin can improve your foreign language vocabulary.
2. Knowing Latin can give you more insight to history and literature.[4]

For example, imagine that you received a notification on your iPhone from Dictionary.com that the word of the day is "sub rosa," which means "confidentially or secretly." The entry would include the following quote from Daniele Vare: "Besides the pleasure of a newly acquired possession, there is an agreeable feeling of having bought it *sub rosa*." Without knowing the meaning of the Latin phrase, you would not fully understand the sentence. Moreover, knowing the derivation of the term helps you to see the rich history of English vocabulary.

The "Origin of Sub Rosa" section of Dictionary.com explains that

> sub rosa comes directly from the Latin phrase *sub rosa*, "under the rose," from the use of a rose suspended from the ceiling of the council chamber meetings to symbolize the sworn confidence of the participants. The use of the rose is based on the Greek myth that Aphrodite (Latin Venus) gave a rose to her son Eros (Latin Cupid); Eros then gave the rose to Harpocrates, the god of silence and secrets, to ensure that Aphrodite's dalliances remained hidden. Sub rosa entered English in the seventeenth century.[5]

Another example of the use of Latin phrases can be found in Joseph McBride's scholarly study of the films of Ernst Lubitsch, *How Did Lubitsch Do It*? Referring to a comment about Lubitsch by the director Billy Wilder, McBride says, "It is also a much-deserved nod to Lubitsch as the precursor, the undisputed primus inter pares among that generation of émigré directors."[6] The Latin phrase "primus inter pares" means "first among equals," and, like many other foreign words used in English texts, such as "émigré," it may or may not be italicized or underlined. In this example, McBride chooses not to use either of those styles. The point is that the meaning of the Latin phrase is essential to understanding McBride's statement about Lubitsch's stature.

In a more general sense, having even a rudimentary knowledge of Latin will aid you in your choice of words in SWAE texts. In the online article "Writers Choose Their Favorite Words," Rebecca Mead states that Latin "underlies half of all English words—including, according to Philip Durkin, chief editor of the Oxford English Dictionary, nearly half of the thousand words most commonly used today."[7] A knowledge of Latin is a window into the fascinating evolution of the English language and the miracle of language acquisition. Latin, therefore, is part of the conservatism and rule adherence fundamental to writers of SWAE. The title of scholar Guy Deutcher's book *The Unfolding of Language: An Evolutionary Tour of Mankind's Greatest Invention* states the case succinctly.[8] As has been pointed out many times in previous chapters, SWAE is a dialect of English that holds writers—and readers—to a very high standard of this wonderful invention.

ESSENTIAL IDEAS IN THIS CHAPTER

- SWAE is essentially about the form of sentences.
- However, sentences are about something, so this is where content comes in.
- Form and content work hand in glove to create meaning.
- SWAE writers are obligated to present content in a responsible and honest way.
- SWAE writers must adhere strictly to the guidelines of academic honesty in attributing credit to their sources.
- A knowledge of Latin will enhance your understanding and use of SWAE.
- Latin is representative of the conservatism and rule adherence of SWAE.

NOTES

1. "The Shape of Content by Ben Shahn," Kirkus Review, https://www.kirkusreviews.com/book-reviews/ben-shahn-3/the-shape-of-content-2/ (accessed October 2, 2017).

2. "Latin Words and Phrases Every Man Should Know," Art of Manliness, https://www.artofmanliness.com/articles/latin-words-and-phrases-every-man-should-know/ (accessed November 12, 2017).

3. Peter R. Macleod, "Latin in Legal Writing: An Inquiry into the Use of Latin in the Modern Legal World." *Boston College Law Review* 39, no. 1 (1998), https://lawdigitalcommons.bc.edu/cgi/viewcontent.cgi?article=2089&context=bclr (accessed November 2017).

4. "Latin Words and Phrases," Art of Manliness.

5. "Sub Rosa," Dictionary.com, https://www.dictionary.com/browse/sub-rosa/ (accessed November 10, 2017).

6. Joseph McBride, *How Did Lubitsch Do It?* (New York: Columbia University Press, 2018), 19.

7. Rebecca Mead, "Writers Choose Their Favorite Words," *New Yorker*, June 11, 2015, https://www.newyorker.com/culture/cultural-comment/writers-choose-their-favorite-words, (accessed October 29, 2017).

8. Guy Deutscher, *The Unfolding of Language: An Evolutionary Tour of Mankind's Greatest Invention* (New York: Henry Holt, 2006).

Epilogue
Consummatum Est

I used the Latin phrase in the title of this final chapter to act as a transition, which is a bridge or connection linking form and content. In effect Latin helps the reader move smoothly from one chapter to another. The phrase *Consummatum est* means "It is finished."

I've tried in this chapter to demonstrate or model the characteristics of SWAE that I've emphasized in the previous chapters:

1. All of the above sentences contain at least one main clause, thus ensuring adherence to Cardinal Rule #1: "All SWAE sentences must contain at least one main clause."
2. The sentences in this chapter—and in all the chapters—demonstrate a variety of sentence patterns: simple, compound, complex, and compound-complex.
3. All of these sentence patterns, among other possibilities, are punctuated correctly

   SC, MC; MC
   MC, cc, MC
   SC, MC, cc MC
   MC; MC

4. I've documented all sources of information that is not my own. It's a crucial characteristic of SWAE that writers must be scrupulous in documenting sources.

I've mentioned above that there are many different types of documentation, depending upon the purpose and the requirements of the organization for which the writing is intended. I've used my own writing to demonstrate how publishers have their own stylebooks and documentation methods. If you were writing an English paper, for example, you would probably be required to use the Modern Language Association (MLA) documentation style. On the other hand, if you were writing a paper for a sociology class, you would be required to conform to the American Psychological Association (APA) style.

5. I've proofread my text in order not to make common errors in SWAE, or in order to correct errors if I had made them. All writers make mistakes; that is why editors—and English teachers—exist. As we've seen in past chapters, errors can disrupt the meaning of texts, or they can distract the reader and undermine communication.

Here is an example from my local newspaper, *The Plain Dealer*: "Giuliani join's Trump's legal team."[1] As I've pointed out above, the apostrophe is involved in a large number of punctuation errors. So pervasive is the problem, that it has been given a name, "the green grocer's apostrophe."

Here is an explanation from the website, *oxforddictionaries.com*:

> This description stems from the fact that green grocers were particularly prone to this error when pricing their produce—we've probably all winced at signs that say 'apple's 80p per pound.' However it's unfair to single out one type of retailer, or even retailers in general, for such mistakes—unfortunately they crop up wherever writing is to be found.

The article goes on to give a clever coinage for this ubiquitous (great SWAE word!) error: "apostroflies."[2]

6. I have tried to support my claim that SWAE writers are held to the highest standard of usage. However, usage, although being the major characteristic of SWAE, is not the whole story of this dialect. There is another element, and that is the content of SWAE texts.

I'd like to provide an excerpt from a recently published scholarly book, written by the eminent historian, Yuval Noah Harari:

> Modern culture rejects this belief in a great cosmic plan. We are not actors in any larger-than-life drama. Life has no script, no playwright, no director, no producer—and no meaning. To the best of our scientific understanding, the universe is a blind and purposeless process, full of sound and fury but signifying nothing. During our infinitesimally brief stay on our tiny speck of a planet, we fret and strut this way and that, and then are heard of no more.[3]

For those of you familiar with what are called, "literary devices," (symbols, similes, personifications, etc.), you will recognize the device being used in this excerpt as a metaphor, an implied comparison between two unalike entities, in this case, life and theater. The purpose of this device is to enlarge the understanding of a topic by bringing in fresh and sometimes surprising comparisons.

An additional characteristic of this excerpt is the use of an allusion (not "illusion"!) to add depth and complexity to an idea. An allusion is another literary device that utilizes a reference to something that exists outside the text being composed. The major sources of allusion in scholarly texts are the Bible, Greek and Roman mythology, and Shakespeare's plays. Well-read readers will recognize the allusion in the above excerpt to Shakespeare's *Macbeth*:

> Tomorrow, and tomorrow, and tomorrow,
> Creeps in this petty pace from day to day
> To the last syllable of recorded time,
> And all our yesterdays have lighted fools
> The way to dusty death. Out, out, brief candle!
> Life's but a walking shadow, a poor player
> That struts and frets his hour upon the stage
> And then is heard no more. It is a tale
> Told by an idiot, full of sound and fury,
> Signifying nothing. (Act V, Scene V, 19–28)

I hope that I have made my case for the significance and importance of SWAE in the context of the English language. Not only is language our greatest invention; it is also the foundation of our culture. Language makes us fully human. And SWAE is the most eloquent expression of this humanity.

NOTES

1. April 20, 2018, A10.
2. "What is the Green Grocer's Apostrophe?" Oxford Dictionaries Blog, https://blog.oxforddictionaries.com/2011/02/04/random-apostrophization/ (accessed November 1, 2017).
3. Yuval Noah Harari. *Homo Deus: A Brief History of Tomorrow* (New York: Harper Perennial, 2017), 201.

Bibliography

American Heritage Dictionary. Boston: Houghton Mifflin Company, 1993.

Auld, Eric K. "A Joke Worth Sharing," *Writing On*. https://writerlingearthling.blogspot.com. Thursday, November 8, 2011.

Baxter, John. *A Pound of Paper: Confessions of a Book Addict*. New York: Thomas Dunne Books, St. Martin's Press, 2002.

Berger, Warren. *A More Beautiful Question: The Power of Inquiry to Spark Breakthrough Ideas*. New York: Bloomsbury USA, 2014.

Bochco, Steven. *Murder in the First*. Second season. TNT.

Chernow, Ron. *Alexander Hamilton*. New York: Penguin Books, 2004.

"Common Knowledge." Online Writing Lab. https://owl.english.purdue.edu/owl/research_and_citation/using_research/avoiding_plagiarism/is_it_plagiarism.html (accessed September 5, 2017).

Crystal, David. *Making a Point: The Persnickety Story of English Punctuation*. New York: St. Martin's Press, 2015.

Crystal, David. *The Stories of English*. Woodstock, NY: Overlook Press, 2004.

Davis, Laura. "Britain's 7 New Social Classes: Do You Fit Into One?" *Independent*, April 3, 2013. https://www.independent.co.uk/voices/ivdrip/britains-7-new-social-classes-do-you-fit-into-one-8558145.html.

Deck, Jeff and Benjamin D. Herson. *The Great Typo Hunt: Two Friends Changing the World One Correction at a Time*. New York: Broadway Books, 2011.

Deutscher, Guy. *The Unfolding of Language: An Evolutionary Tour of Mankind's Greatest Invention*. New York: Henry Holt and Co., 2006.

"French Academy: French Literary Organization." *Encyclopedia Britannica*. http://www.britannica.com/topic/French-Academy (accessed December 1, 2017).

"Giuliani Join's Trump's Legal Team." *Plain Dealer*. April 20, 2018, A10.

Harari, Yuval Noah. *Homo Deus: A Brief History of Tomorrow*. New York: Harper Perennial, 2017.

James, Henry. *Portrait of a Lady*. New York: Macmillan and Company, Ltd., 1881.

Kalb, Peggy. "Why 'Bad' English Isn't." *Yale Alumni Magazine*, July/August 2013. https://yalealumnimagazine.com/articles/3716.

Kirsch, Adam. "How to Live with Critics (Whether You're an Artist or the President)." *New York Times*, June 14, 2017. https://www.nytimes.com/2017/06/14/books/review/how-to-live-with-critics.html.

"Lack of Comma Could Cost Maine Company Millions in Overtime Dispute." *New York Times*, March 16, 2017. https://www.nytimes.com/2017/03/16/us/oxford-commalawsuit.html.

"Latin in Legal Writing: An Inquiry into the Use of Latin in the Modern Legal World." *Boston College Law Review*, 1998. https://lawdigitalcommons.bc.edu/bclr/vol39/iss1/6 (accessed November 2017).

"Latin Words and Phrases Every Man Should Know." Art of Manliness. https://www.artofmaliness.com/articles/latin-words-and-phrases-every-man-should-know/ (accessed November 12, 2017).

Lesbian, Gay, Bisexual, Transgender Resource Center. "Gendered Pronouns." University of Wisconsin at Milwaukee. https://uwm.edu/lgbtrc/support/gender-pronouns? (accessed November 15, 2017).

Marquis, Don. "mehitabel s morals." https://tuitalk.wordpress.com/2011/05/10/tuesday-poem-mehitabel-s-morals-by-don-marquis/ (accessed December 5, 2017).

McBride. Joseph. *How Did Lubitsch Do It?* New York: Columbia U Press, 2018.

Mead, Rebecca. "Writers Choose Their Favorite Words." *New Yorker*, June 11, 2014. https://www.newyorker.com/culture/cultural-comment/writers-choose-their-favorite-words.

Merriam-Webster Online Dictionary. https://www.merriam-webster.com (accessed November 12, 2017).

"Noah Webster and America's First Dictionary." Merriam-Webster. https://merriam-webster.com/info/noah.htm (accessed November 15, 2017).

Norris, Mary. *Between You and Me: Confessions of a Comma Queen*. New York: W. W. Norton & Company, 2015.

Oberg, Rebecca. "Using Sentence Fragments Wisely." http://www.sophia.org/tutorials/using-sentence-fragments-wisely (accessed December 10, 2017).

"Only in America." *The Week*. 10 August, 2018, 6.

Purdue Online Writing Lab (OWL). https://owl.English.purdue.edu/owl/resource/589/02 (accessed November 16, 2017).

"*The Shape of Content* by Ben Shahn." *Kirkus Reviews*. https://www.kirkusreviews.com/book-reviews/ben-shahn-3/the-shape-of-Content-2/ (accessed October 2, 2017).

Shore, Esther. *Bridge of Words: Esperanto and the Dream of a Universal Language*. New York: Metropolitan Books, 2016.

Skerry, Philip, and Amelia Babin Horvat. *That Pesky S: A Jed Simon Grammar Mystery*. Cleveland: Sidestreet Press, 2018.

Stamper, Kory. *Word by Word: The Secret Life of Dictionaries*. New York: Pantheon Books, 2017.

"Sub rosa." Dictionary.com. https://www.dictionary.com/browse/sub-rosa/ (accessed November 10, 2017).

"Subject and Verb Agreement with Collective Nouns." GrammarBook.com. https://data.grammarbook.com/blog/singular-vs-plural/subject-and-verb-agreement-with-collective-nouns/ (accessed October 2, 2017).

"Themselves." Lexico. https://www.lexico.com/definition/themselves (accessed October 15, 2017).

Truss, Lynne. *Eats, Shoots and Leaves: The Zero Tolerance Approach to Punctuation.* New York: Gotham, 2003.

Truss, Lynne. *Girl's Like Spaghetti: Why, You Can't Manage Without Apostrophes!* New York: G. P. Putnam, 2007.

Twain, Mark. *The Adventures of Huckleberry Finn.* New York: Chatto and Windus, 1885.

Webster's Third New International Dictionary of the English Language Unabridged. Springfield, MA: G. & C. Merriam Company, 1961.

"What Is the Green Grocer's Apostrophe?" Oxford Dictionaries. https://blog.oxforddictionaries.com/2011/02/04/random-apostrophization/ (accessed November 1, 2017; site discontinued).

www.ingramcontent.com/pod-product-compliance
Lightning Source LLC
Chambersburg PA
CBHW030145240426
43672CB00005B/280